FILM SCHEDULING FILM BUDGETING

WORKBOOK

RALPH S. SINGLETON

LONE EAGLE

THE CONVERSATION reprinted in its entirety with permission from Francis F. Coppola.

THE FILM SCHEDULING / FILM BUDGETING WORKBOOK

LONE EAGLE PUBLISHING
9903 Santa Monica Blvd - Suite 204
Beverly Hills, CA 90212

Printed in the United States of America

Cover designed by Gloriane Harris

Typesetting by Communigraphics, Inc., Los Angeles, California

ISBN 0-943728-07-X

NOTE: The names, addresses, figures; etc., which are contained in the sample forms are for information and example purposes only. They are not to be construed as actual forms used during the making of *THE CONVERSATION.*

TABLE OF CONTENTS

ACKNOWLEDGMENTS

I am extremely grateful to Francis Coppola for his generosity in allowing me to use his wonderful screenplay, *THE CONVERSATION*, in its entirety. Without his permission and cooperation, this book and its companions could never have been possible.

A special thanks to Steve Goepel, Michael Kennedy, Jim Turner and Joan Vietor for their assistance in designing the budget form.

INTRODUCTION

The **Film Scheduling / Film Budgeting Workbook** has been designed as part of a complete course (or do-it-yourself) on professional motion picture production.

When I wrote **Film Scheduling** and **Film Budgeting**, I wanted to base all my examples on a screenplay of a feature film project that had actually been produced. I wanted you to be able to read the books, follow the examples and create your own production boards and budgets, and then have a chance to be able to see the finished film as it was released. Seeing a film that you have "worked on" — even to the extent of doing these examples — is exciting! We were very fortunate to be able to include *Francis Coppola's* Academy Award nominated screenplay, *THE CONVERSATION*, in its entirety. It is a masterfully written screenplay, intriguing and interesting in its designed complexity. Although the film is not presently in release, it does show at "art houses," and is probably available for rent on video-cassette. I would strongly urge you to see *THE CONVERSATION*, after you have finished your board and budget. You will find it an extremely rewarding experience, especially in terms of seeing what actually made it to the screen from the final draft script which is included here.

SCENE NUMBER / DAY NUMBER INDEX
In preparing this series of books, I found that there were times I would need to know, for example, what day the Catholic Church sequence was shot. I could always refer to the board or shooting schedule, but found it was simpler to check a Scene Number / Day Number Index which I'd created. I've included it for you, but don't get in the habit of relying on it. Try to create your own schedule. Use the one laid out in **Film Scheduling** as an example, but then go on and create your own.

SAMPLE PRODUCTION FORMS
Originally, I had planned to include copies of the various forms which are currently in use by the studios and are available at local stationers. However, when I assembled them, I found that there was no cohesiveness — and that many were extremely out-dated. Some hadn't been changed in over thirty years! So, the ones included here have all been re-designed. These forms are not to be photocopied — there is another book, just for that: **Movie Production & Budget Forms . . . Instantly!** That book contains the production and budget forms, but not the script of *THE CONVERSATION*. The format is a little larger so that when you photocopy it, you won't get our page numbers and headings, etc. — you'll just get clean, readable forms. The forms in this workbook are made for you to work on, so take out your pen and fill them in. Don't worry about marking in this book — that's what it's made for.

SAMPLE BUDGET FORM
Again, as with the production forms, there really wasn't a budget form available that I found to be adequate. The ones that the major studios use are better than the ones available to the independents, but they still had their problems. And what good would it be to show you a budget on a form that you could never use? You won't find 20th Century Fox's budget form for sale anywhere. The solution to this problem was to design a form that was comprehensive, but not too overwhelming. I looked at at least 10 different budget forms ranging in size from 14 pages to 100 pages. I saw similarities among them— some for no reason at all. Why did the Electricians have their own department and not the Grips, who were listed under "Set Operations?". . this didn't make sense. Also, Location Expenses covered those expenses for a *distant* location, but what happens if your location is local? Those expenses had also been lumped under Set Operations. So, now the Grips have their own, Grip Department, and Location Expenses are divided into Location Expenses and Site Rental.

All of this, and more, is explained in detail in **Film Budgeting** and **Film Scheduling**.

NOT JUST FOR 35MM
Although the thrust of this book is for *professional* feature productions, the concepts and forms can be used for 16mm and 8mm productions, too. The budgets won't have to be as detailed and you probably won't need all the production forms, but you will definitely find it is easier to eliminate a category from this budget form that it is to create one from scratch.

SIX EASY STEPS
If you are going to take this DO-IT-YOURSELF course on film production on your own, here are the six steps that I recommend you follow:

1. Read **Film Scheduling.**
2. Breakdown *THE CONVERSATION* and prepare your own production budget and shooting schedule.
3. Read **Film Budgeting.**
4. Complete the budget form in **The Film Scheduling / Film Budgeting Workbook.**
5. Understand all the sample production forms in **The Film Scheduling/Film Budgeting Workbook**, and fill them in yourself.
6. Try your own feature script. Use **Movie Production & Budget Forms . . . Instantly!** for your own forms.

Nothing can replace years of experience; however, having gone through the steps of preparing a production board and accurate budget can only stand you in good stead in your quest for a career in the motion picture industry, which is why, I presume you bought these books. I can't promise that you will be able to get a job by reading these books, but I can assure you that you will have a good skill under your belt.

I'd enjoy hearing from you — your successes, your criticisms, your suggestions. You can send them to me in care of my publisher — the address is on the copyright page.

Good luck! Let's make movies!

Ralph S. Singleton
Beverly Hills

August 1984

THE CONVERSATION

THE CONVERSATION

Original Screenplay by
FRANCIS FORD COPPOLA

THE DIRECTOR'S COMPANY
827 Folsom Street
San Francisco, California

Final Draft
November 22, 1972

Francis Ford Coppola's THE CONVERSATION

---

1 FADE IN: 1
EXT. UNION SQUARE - DAY

MEDIUM VIEW

A band of street musicians have just set up in the park. Clarinet, trombone, banjo, saxophone and trumpet. They wear fragments of velvet and silk, pieces of old uniforms and odd-ball hats. They haven't yet attracted a crowd. One of them takes a top hat from his head, puts it on the ground and then throws a few coins and bills into it. Then the band breaks into a jazz rendition of "Red, Red, Robin." 3/8

---

2 HIGH FULL VIEW 2

December in San Francisco. The Downtown area, centering around Union Square. Christmas decorations are already up, the electricity turned on in the middle of the afternoon. The crowds of shoppers have swelled with office workers out for their lunch hour. 2/8

---

3 SUPERIMPOSE MAIN TITLE AND CREDIT TITLES 3

over this view as it begins a very slow zoom in on the park. The titles take about as much time as the zoom so they are ready to conclude just as we have centered on a close view of a Young Mime dressed as a Drum Major. He has a slight crowd drawn around him as he imitates certain unsuspecting people as they come down a park walkway. He is very good, and usually gets a round of applause for his imitation. 2/8

---

4 CLOSE VIEW OF THE MUSICIANS 4

One of them puts down his instrument and does a rollicking tap dance. DANCER? OR DANCE DIRECTOR? 1/8

---

5 CLOSER VIEW 5

The tap shoes step out rhythms near the top hat. 1/8

---

6 VIEW ON THE MIME 6

Imitating a middle-aged, slow, bobbing walk. But precise and purposeful. He sips coffee out of an imaginary cup. 1/8

---

7 THE VIEW ALTERS 7

revealing the subject: a rather ordinary-looking man in his middle forties with a thin moustache*, dressed immaculately in an out-of-fashion suit, with a slow, bobbing walk. He sips coffee from a steaming cardboard cup wrapped in a paper bag. THIS IS HARRY CAUL. 2/8

---

8 VIEW ON THE MUSICIANS 8

The saxophonist blares a raspy solo to everyone's delight, especially Harry's. He stops for a moment, appreciatively, as they go into the last chorus of "Red, Red Robin."

9 EXT. UNION SQUARE - DAY 9

A young couple pass in front of Harry for a moment, obscuring him from OUR VIEW. She is in her early twenties, girlish and very pretty, bundled against the cold, foggy afternoon. Her name is ANN, and she holds tightly the arm of a clean cut young man about 26. He's dressed nicely with the look of a fraternity boy: his name is MARK. They join the group of spectators around the band.

ANN
"...Wake up, wake up you sleepy head, Get up, get up, get out of bed..."

OUR VIEW PANS around the group of people, some listening to the band, others passing by. Occasionally even fragments of a disinterested Harry Caul behind them. As we single out particular people, we catch fragments of what they are saying.

ANN
"...Cheer up, cheer up..."

A YOUNG MAN
...Are you going to see...

A WOMAN
...Really, they're both coming.
I think I'll tell...

THE VIEW returns to Ann just as she's asking Mark for something to throw into the top hat.

ANN
You got a quarter?

Mark tosses a coin into the top hat as the two continue on their walk, OUR VIEW moving with them, leaving Harry with the band.

(CONTINUED)

9 CONTINUED: 9

ANN
...What do you think? I don't know what to get him for Christmas, he's already got everything.

MARK
He doesn't need anything... anymore.

ANN
I haven't decided.

Some people block OUR VIEW temporarily; her voice cuts out. Now we SEE them again, but we HEAR only static and then TOTAL SILENCE, as though something has gone wrong with the sound track. Then it is corrected:

ANN
...what about me?

MARK
You'll see.

ANN
You're no fun. You're supposed to tease me, give me hints, you know.

Ann slows by a green bench, where an old derelict is asleep, bundled up in an overcoat, wearing big black shoes with no socks under them.

ANN
Look, that's terrible.

MARK
He's not hurting anyone.

They continue their walk, moving further away from us. But oddly enough, their voices remain clear and in the foreground. We notice they pass Harry, who is now sitting on one of the benches. After they pass, he rises and quickly crosses the street and moves down the steps of the park toward a small panel van truck with a large sign: "PIONEER GLASS AND MIRROR COMPANY" printed above the two mirrors mounted on the side. As Harry moves toward the van, we HEAR the following:

ANN (o.s.)
Every time I see one of them I always think the same thing.

(CONTINUED)

9 CONTINUED: 9

MARK (o.s.)
What do you think?

ANN (o.s.)
I think he was somebody's baby.
Don't laugh, really I do.

OUR VIEW moves up the face of the building, up to the roof, where it comes to rest on a neon Eiffel Tower lit in the daylight with the large letters: "CITY OF PARIS." There, we can clearly see a man bundled in a warm quilted coat holding a five-foot extended shotgun microphone with a gunsight on it. He wears headphones.

ANN (o.s.)
I think he was somebody's baby
boy and they loved him...
and here he is now, half-dead on
a park bench.

10 THIS MAN'S VIEW 10

From this height, the people in Union Square are tiny and unrecognizable.

ANN (o.s.)
...and where is his mother or
his father or his uncles?

11 VIEW THROUGH THE GUN SIGHT 11

A very clear CLOSE-UP of Ann, with the cross-hairs right on her mouth.

ANN
Anyway, that's what I always
think.

She looks at Mark.

CUT TO:

12 INT. THE MIRROR VAN - DAY 12

Seated at a work bench, over a rack of professional tape-recorders is a young technician wearing earphones. His eyeglasses have been temporarily mended with a Band-Aid holding the frame together. His name is STANLEY.

(CONTINUED)

12 CONTINUED: 12

MARK (o.s.)
I guess I think of how when they
had a newspaper strike in New York,
more of those old drunks died in
one night...

There is a knock on the door. Stan takes off the headset, discontinuing Mark's discussion. He reaches over and undoes the van latch. Quickly, Harry Caul steps in, closes the door, and moves to the opposite side of the van, to one of the two tinted windows. One can see through to the outside. He picks up a set of binoculars and looks outside toward the park where Mark and Ann are walking and talking.

CUT TO:

13 EXT. THE VAN - DAY 13

The Glass and Mirror Company van, harmlessly parked in the city.

Two pretty secretaries on their way to lunch, crossing the street, pause in front of the large mirrors, fixing their make-up.

CUT TO:

14 INT. THE VAN - DAY 14

Harry is annoyed with the girls primping in front of his view. He stands impatiently with the binoculars in his hands. Stanley laughs and swivels in his chair and quickly snaps pictures of them with a motorized camera.

STANLEY
C'mon little babies, c'mon, lick your
lips (snap) wet your lips (snap,
snap, snap).

15 CLOSE ON THE SECRETARIES 15

(through the one-way glass). Wetting and smoothing their lipstick.

STAN (o.s.)
C'mon, gimme some tongue (snap,
snap, snap.)

CUT TO:

16 MEDIUM VIEW 16

Harry stands patiently with his binoculars. Stan is snapping off shots.

STAN
Stick it out, gimme a nice wet French kiss...(snap, snap)

HARRY
Pay attention to the recording, will you?

Stan puts the headset back on.

STAN
Coming in loud and clear.

Harry indicates that he wants the headset; it's given to him and Harry listens carefully.

ANN (o.s.)
That's terrible.

MARK (o.s.)
Who started this conversation anyhow?

ANN (o.s.)
You did.

MARK (o.s.)
I did not.

ANN (o.s.)
You did, too, you just don't remember.

STANLEY
Who's so interested in these two?

HARRY
Don't know for sure.

STANLEY
The Justice Department?

HARRY
No.

STANLEY
Then I figure it's the Infernal Revenue people; their recording's putting me to sleep.

(CONTINUED)

16 CONTINUED: 16

HARRY
(smiling)
Since when you supposed to be entertained?

STANLEY
Sometimes it's nice to know what they're talking about.

HARRY
(half to himself)
I don't care what they're talking about. I just want a nice fat recording.
(indicates headset)
How you doing?

STANLEY
We're getting better than 40 percent.

HARRY
How about the second position.

STANLEY
Not so good.

Stanley turns the dial up on the second recorder, and for a moment, the conversation is doubled up on itself.

CUT TO:

17 EXT. TOP OF THE CITY OF PARIS - DAY 17

THE VIEW PANS from the man under the Eiffel Tower sign across the park, to another man operating out of an open window of an office building. He is operating a second microphone identical to the first one we saw. It becomes clear that the young couple are being tracked from opposing positions. We HEAR the young man laughing.

18 VIEW ON THE COUPLE 18

MARK
Where'd you hear that?

ANN
(also laughing)
My secret.

CUT TO:

19 VIEW ON THE MIME 19

He laughs, as he does a burlesque of the two of them walking for an amused crowd.

20 MOVING VIEW OF MARK AND ANN 20

Ignorant of the Mime, still walking.

MARK
How do you feel?

ANN
Oh, you know.

21 OUR VIEW MOVES 21

from the two of them to another man walking rather near to them, carrying a shopping bag and reading a newspaper.

22 CLOSE VIEW 22

The man with the shopping bag is wearing a hearing aid.

MARK
It's a nice day today; yesterday it was cold and foggy.

ANN
Do you...(CUTS OUT)

We notice the man with the shopping bag has let too many people get between them. He walks quickly to make up the gap, catching fragments of other people's conversations: Waiting for you..." "Can't do it, but..." "...I was really...."

Finally, he succeeds in making it back, close to them.

MARK
I'm tired of drinking anyhow. I'm tired of mostly everything.

ANN
Tired of me?

MARK
(Static)....you. But not today.

(CONTINUED)

22 CONTINUED: 22

She smiles at Mark, affectionately, but in the course of her look catches a glimpse of the man with the shopping bag. An expression of fear comes to her face. The man senses this, and coolly continues past them, paying no further attention.

23 EXT. OFFICE BUILDING - DAY 23

The man operating the long microphone out of the open window moves his microphone sights.

CUT TO:

24 TELESCOPIC VIEW 24

Centers on Ann's face as she moves closer to Mark, and whispers:

ANN
Look. See him? The one with the hearing aid...like...

MARK
No. Where?

ANN
He was following us. He kept following us close.

She touches Mark's arm; she squeezes it.

MARK
It's nothing; don't worry about it.

For a moment it seems as though Ann is going to cry, but she avoids it.

ANN
God, it will be so good to be finished with this.

They round the corner, turning their backs to our telescopic VIEW, and the sound becomes muffled and undiscernible.

CUT TO:

25 EXT. EIFFEL TOWER BUILDING - DAY 25

The man working under the neon Eiffel Tower scans the field through his telescopic sight, searching for his subjects.

CUT TO:

26 TELESCOPIC VIEW 26

The cross-hairs swish over an out-of-focus moving image, catching fragments of people and buildings and now comes to rest on the two targets. When it finds their mouths, we can hear them again. They are standing by a group of fellows playing bongo drums. The sound of the drums interferes with the track.

MARK
...he'd...(the bongos are distorting the track)...chance...

ANN
You know he records the telephones...

MARK
We'd better get back, it's almost two.

ANN
(as they move away from the drums)
Please don't go back there, please, not until...(she doesn't finish her sentence.)

MARK
Alright. I won't.

27 INT. THE MIRROR VAN - DAY 27

Stan operates the recorders; Harry's listening through the headset while sipping a steaming paper cup of coffee. There's another knock on the van door; Stanley opens the door a crack and lets the man with the shopping bag into the van. He is tall, middle-aged: PAUL MEYERS.

He takes his hearing aid off and pulls out a small transmitter and a directional microphone out of the shopping bag. He's apparently been out there a while and is a little cold.

PAUL
I got burnt, Harry, she looked at me. Sorry.

HARRY
I heard. How'd you do?

(CONTINUED)

27 CONTINUED: 27

PAUL
Not bad. I got pieces, good pieces. Maybe 2Ø, 25 percent.

HARRY
Good. Feel like some coffee?

PAUL
No, thanks. (Looking around the van) Something else, maybe.

Harry leans forward and gets a small pint of whiskey, offers it to him. Paul takes a sip.

PAUL
That's good.

HARRY
Thanks, Paul. I'll call you if anything else comes up.

Harry pays him in cash, which he quickly puts away in his billfold.

PAUL
I go on duty in an hour. So long, fellas.

Paul leaves the van. Harry picks up the headset and listens to the conversation once again.

STANLEY
That Paul, he's a helluva nice guy...you know, for a cop.

We SEE the afternoon traffic passing through the two-way window.

MARK
I'll stay here a while.

ANN (o.s.)
Goodbye. Wait, you have something in your eye.

CUT TO:

28 EXT. UNION SQUARE - DAY 28

The crowds have thinned out now that the lunch hour is over. The young couple have just parted. Ann

(CONTINUED:

28 CONTINUED: 28

hurries over towards Powell Street, casting one look after Mark. Mark turns, sits on a bench, watches her for a moment. Not far from him, the groggy bum awakens, looking around at the day. Soon, Ann has disappeared. Mark stands up, tosses his lunch-bag away, and moves in the opposite direction.

CUT TO:

29 INT. THE MIRROR VAN - DAY 29

Stanley fast rewinds the recorders, putting away the headsets. Harry waits quietly, leaning against the glass.

STANLEY
What's the matter Harry? You're awfully hinky today, all nerves. What's bothering you?

HARRY
(sharply)
Mind your own business, Stanley.

A long pause, and then Harry breaks out into laughter.

HARRY
(laughing to himself)
Mind your own business.

Stan looks at him totally confused, and then it comes to him.

STANLEY
Mind your own business!! Oh, Harry! Oh, Harry!

CUT TO:

30 EXT. THE MIRROR CO. VAN - DAY 30

Parked innocently by the curb. We HEAR the muffled sound of laughter coming from within.

CUT TO:

31 EXT. THE EIFFEL TOWER BUILDING - DAY 31

The man begins to disassemble the long microphone into sections, putting each piece into a nylon bag with a pull-string.

CUT TO:

32 EXT. OFFICE BUILDING - DAY 32

The man packs the disassembled equipment into two large suitcases while whistling to himself.

CUT TO:

33 EXT. UNION SQUARE - DAY 33

The street band of musicians are putting their instruments into felt bags, and then into the instrument cases. One of them takes the top hat and tips the money out of it.

FADE OUT:

FADE IN:

34 EXT. THE ELECTRIC BUS - DAY 34

MOVING VIEW
The bus moves silently along the avenue, its large feeler resting upwards against the high voltage wires.

CUT TO:

35 INT. THE ELECTRIC BUS - DAY 35

Harry sits in the middle of the bus; one of many tired people on their way home from work. The bus rounds a corner, there's a thumping sound and it stops dead. The passengers seem to know what it is and deal with it in a casual way. The non-plussed driver hops up, moves outside with big steps, and expertly begins to pull the cables to reset the connection. Harry becomes impatient and steps off the bus.

36 EXT. THE NEIGHBORHOOD - DAY 36

The big black rods jam around the wires, spilling electricity all around the street, as Harry walks the last few blocks to his home.

37 MOVING VIEW ON HARRY 37

Bobbing down the street, while the bus, connected once again, pulls up silently behind him, and then passes him as he crosses the street.

CUT TO:

38 INT. NEIGHBORHOOD MARKET - DAY 38

Harry moves down the aisle of the little market, picking out a single tomato, a cellophane wrapped packet of pork chops, a single can of beer, and takes it all to the man at the counter.

CUT TO:

39 INT. A LAUNDRY - DAY 39

A woman moves down a counter of laundry packages, while her little boy sits amazed watching Harry make a glass full of water disappear under a dishtowel, badly.

WOMAN
(looking for his packages)
Harry Caul, Harry Caul...Harry Caul.

BOY
Tell me.

HARRY
A magician never tells his secrets.

BOY
You can tell me.

HARRY
It's a secret...and when it stops being a secret it's not anything.

WOMAN
Harry Caul: 5 shirts, 6 underwear, 5 pairs of socks.

Harry smiles, takes the packages and leaves.

BOY
So long, Harry.

4Ø INT. APARTMENT BUILDING - DAY 4Ø

Harry enters the hallway of the apartment, all bronze-yellow. He takes out his personal mail key, and opens his mailbox.

There are some bills, some advertisements, and a greeting card. He begins up the stairs when a neighbor woman passes him with her dog.

(CONTINUED)

40 CONTINUED: 40

HARRY
Hello.

WOMAN
Hello, Mr. Caul.

He is halfway up the stairs when she turns and adds:

And HAPPY BIRTHDAY!

Harry nods pleasantly, but this puzzles him.

CUT TO:

41 INT. HARRY'S FLOOR - DAY 41

He arrives at his floor, unlocks his apartment door, which has two latches. It opens part way and we hear a slight thud. Harry peeks behind the door and finds a gaily-wrapped wine bottle fallen on its side. He closes the door and picks the card from the ribbon. "Happy Birthday Harry"--Maria Evangelista.

HARRY
(muttering to himself)
Happy Birthday Harry, Happy Birthday
Harry, (while dialing on his phone)
Happy Birthday Harry...
Hello? Mrs. Evangelista?
Yes. Harry Caul. Yes, yes, thanksalot
I found it, yes...You're really nice.
Yes, thank you Mrs. Evangelista, but
what I wanted to know was how did you
put it in my apartment?

(silence)
I thought I had the only key. I know
that. But what emergency could possibly...
all right, I'd be perfectly happy to have
my personal things burnt up in a fire.
Anyway, I don't have any personal things.
Nothing of value; nothing personal.
Except my key, which I'd like to have the
only copy of.

He's been looking through his mail as he conducts this conversation; he looks over at the greeting card and it has the message printed with certain information handwritten in: "To our valued customer (handwritten) Harry, Happy Birthday, here's to another (handwritten) 44. The Security Pacific Bank".

(CONTINUED)

41 CONTINUED: 41

How'd you know it was my birthday?
(silence)
I don't remember telling you. Can you guess how old I am? 44? Very good guess, Mrs. Evangelista. By the way, from today on, my mail will go to a Post Office box, with a combination and no key! Goodbye.

Harry hangs up.

Happy Birthday, Harry.

CUT TO:

42 INT. KITCHENETTE - NIGHT 42

Two scrawny porkchops are frying; Harry is slicing the tomato. He HEARS some muffled voices coming from the next apartment and then some shouting.

HARRY
(muttering to himself)
What is this? Grand Central Station.

He takes the porkchops out of the pan. The voices persist, but we cannot understand what they are saying. He ignores them a moment more, moves to the wall, and puts his ear up against it. He moves to the counter, takes a water glass and holding it up against the wall, listens through that.

Still unsuccessful, he moves away, takes a hardback chair and carries it into a little closet. Puts the chair up in the closet, takes a broom-stick, and standing up on the chair, uses the broom-stick to push up on a small maintenance trapdoor in the closet ceiling.

We can hear the voices more clearly now: an argument.

MAN (o.s.)
GODDAMN LANDLORD!

WOMAN (o.s.)
Stop shouting, or I'll close the windows.

There's a knock at Harry's door; he quickly takes the chair out of the closet.

(CONTINUED)

42 CONTINUED: 42

HARRY
One minute.

He gets rid of any eavesdropping evidence, and opens the door. An angry young man stands there staring at him, RON KELLER.

RON
Excuse me, we haven't met, but do you have any water?

HARRY
I....don't know.

RON
I'm a new tenant here, and I don't have any water and I wonder if you'd check to see if you have any.

MR. CORSITTO (o.s.)
What's the matter with the water?

Another tenant has poked his head out of his door.

MR. CORSITTO
Last week there was no hot water. Now there's no water at all.

RON
This is the last straw.

While this discussion is going on down the hall, Harry deftly closes his door trying not to be involved. Just as he gets it closed, there's another knock. He opens it and there's another tenant, BOB, smiling who seems to know him better. Ron is still angrily debating the matter with Mr. Corsitto.

BOB
Hiya, Harry. You, too, eh?

HARRY
Yeah, it's...

BOB
The heat's screwed up, the plumbing. We could probably call the Health Department because of the water in the basement.

(CONTINUED)

42 CONTINUED: 42

Bob peeks into Harry's apartment the whole time he talks which makes Harry uncomfortable, so he steps out into the hallway pulling the door semi-closed behind him while listening.

CUT TO:

43 INT. HARRY'S FLOOR HALLWAY - DAY 43

BOB'S WIFE (o.s.)
Bob, where are you?

BOB
(calling out)
Up here with Harry Caul.

BOB'S WIFE (o.s.)
Is his water off, too?

Ron Keller, without having been invited, has stepped into Harry's apartment and tested the water.

RON
This apartment has water.

Harry's a bit surprised to see Ron in his apartment and moves back into it. Bob accompanies him.

CUT TO:

44 INT. HARRY'S APARTMENT - DAY 44

BOB
Oh this is Ron Keller, a new tenant. This is Harry Caul.

RON
Pleased to meet you, Harry. We're paying good rent here. What about a rent strike? By the way, Happy Birthday, Harry.

HARRY
Thanks.

BOB
(testing the water for himself)
How come only one apartment has water?

(CONTINUED)

44 CONTINUED: 44

Now Bob's wife and Mr. Corsitto enter.

HARRY
Why don't we all go down to Mrs. Evangelista's apartment. We'll complain...

BOB
Nothing happens when you complain to her.

RON
I'm for a rent strike.

BOB
It's not the old woman's fault. But she won't get tough with him.

HARRY
Tough with who?

BOB
We don't know, exactly.

RON
With the landlord, of course!

In the distance we hear a female voice.

MRS. GOETNER (o.s.)
Happy Birthday to you,
Happy Birthday to you...

Harry closes his eyes in disbelief as:

BOB
It's Harry's birthday.

BOB'S WIFE
Yes, I heard, Mrs. Goetner.
Happy Birthday, Happy Birthday.

When he opens his eyes, Mrs. Goetner has arrived with her dog and half a pound cake with some candles improvised.

MRS. GOETNER
I thought a party was going on.
A birthday party!

(CONTINUED)

44 CONTINUED: 44

HARRY
No, actually we were discussing...

BOB'S WIFE
Blow out the candle, Mr. Caul, for good luck.

RON
Yeah, like maybe we'll get some water in this place.

They laugh. Harry reluctantly blows out the candle. Everyone oohs and aahs. Mr. Corsitto has returned, still wrapping a spur of the moment gift.

MR. CORSITTO
This...is just a little something.

HARRY
(quite distracted by the many people looking around his apartment.)
Thanks...really...

Mr. Corsitto nods that Harry should unwrap it, and he does. It is a plastic Madonna.

MR. CORSITTO
I've noticed you at Mass, Mr. Caul, on Sunday. It's for your car.

HARRY
I don't really have a car, but I'll keep it in my room. Thanks very much.

Bob is leaning over the tenor saxophone that rests on a stand.

BOB
You a musician, Harry?

HARRY
No...I...

RON
I think we ought to pick a tenants' representative.

HARRY
...play a little.

(CONTINUED)

44 CONTINUED: 44

RON
...and send him straight to
the landlord.

MR. CORSITTO
I would go, but you know I have
difficulty with speaking good,
you know, with the language.

BOB'S WIFE
Well, Mr. Caul has been here the
longest.

HARRY
(catching the drift of
the conversation)
Me, I don't ...

BOB
Yeah, that's a good idea, Harry.

RON
How about it?

Pause. All these people are looking at Harry, standing around in his apartment. He'd do anything to get rid of them.

HARRY
Well...alright. I'll be the Tenant's
Representative, if someone gets me the
address.

RON
It's all handled by some lawyer's
office. I'll take care of that.

The group seems to be satisfied. Harry tries to usher them out, instinctively preventing someone from peeking into this or looking at that.

HARRY
I really have to go. I have to be
somewhere in half an hour.

BOB'S WIFE
A birthday party, I hope.

(CONTINUED)

44 CONTINUED: 44

HARRY
Yes...with my family.

MR. CORSITTO
Do you have family in town, Mr. Caul?
That's very good.

He gradually ushers them all out of his apartment, all saying "goodbye" and "Happy Birthday" and "how nice that he has family."

CUT TO:

45 EXT. THE ELECTRIC BUS - NIGHT 45

Harry is one of the few passengers as the oddly silent bus moves through the fog. It stops and he gets off, crosses a lonely street and enters a building. We notice that he is carrying his birthday wine.

CUT TO:

46 INT. THE BUILDING - NIGHT 46

Harry stands at the base of the staircase, looking up. He waits there a moment, almost hiding, and then continues up the stairs. He approaches the apartment door very, very quietly. He takes a key out, not making a sound, then opens the door quickly and looks into the room.

VOICE
Harry.

CUT TO:

47 INT. THE ROOM - NIGHT 47

We can see through the open door. The room is semi lit, and small. There are a few personal things around in it; a small stereo on the floor, some photographs on the walls, but there is a feeling of impermanence about the room. A girl half-rises from a bed in the corner of the room; she has pale skin, perhaps 24 or 25 with curly hair, sort of pretty. She has fallen asleep in a faded silk Oriental robe. Her name is AMY.

(CONTINUED)

47 CONTINUED 47

AMY
I didn't think you were coming.

Harry closes the door behind him.

HARRY
Just for a while.

AMY
Oh.

HARRY
I brought this wine. Someone gave me a birthday present.

AMY
I didn't know it was your birthday.

She seems half-asleep, but genuinely happy that he has come.

HARRY
I should have called.

Amy slips back under the covers. There is something frightened and very vulnerable about her.

AMY
(not reproachfully)
You never do.

HARRY
You should go out more.

AMY
You don't like me to.

HARRY
I don't mind.

AMY
Then I wouldn't be here if you came over.

HARRY.
Want some wine?

Amy nods. Then she smiles.

AMY
Harry, how old are you?

(CONTINUED)

47 CONTINUED: 47

He moves to the kitchenette, starts to open the wine bottle.

HARRY
Forty-four.

AMY
You're almost twice as old as me. That's sweet, when you were my age, I was being born. Sweet.

Harry gives her a glass of wine. She clinks it to his and they each take a sip.

AMY
Does something special happen between us on your birthday?

HARRY
Like what?

AMY
Something personal?

HARRY
Like what?

AMY
Like...telling me about yourself. Your secrets.

Harry smiles.

HARRY
I don't have any secrets.

AMY
(looks at him knowingly)
I'm your secret, Harry.
(brightly)
Where do you live? Why can't I call you there?

HARRY
(lying)
I don't...have a telephone.

(CONTINUED)

47 CONTINUED: 47

AMY

But you DO have secrets, Harry, I know. Sometimes you come here; but you don't let me know. Once I saw you down by the staircase, hiding. For a whole hour.

This embarrasses Harry; but she keeps on teasing him.

I think you're jealous. You think you're going to catch me at something. Sweet.

(she sips)

The only thing you'll ever catch me at is waiting for you.

(she laughs)

You have a way of opening the door when you come here. You sneak up, very quiet, like a mouse. Then the door opens real fast, just like you think you're going to catch me at something. At first I used to think that it was a fireman coming to warn me that the building was on fire.

(sincerely)

Oh, Harry, how could you ever be jealous of me?

HARRY

I'm not jealous.

AMY

Sometimes I even think you're listening to me. When I'm talking on the telephone. I just feel that you're listening to me.

HARRY

(uncomfortable)

What are you talking about?

AMY

What do you do all day, Harry?

HARRY

I work

AMY

Where?

CONTINUED:

47 CONTINUED: 47

HARRY
I have my own business.

AMY
What kind of business.

HARRY
I don't like people to ask me
a lot of questions.

He's irritated. He gets up and disappears into the bathroom. He HOLD on the closed door for a moment.

AMY (o.s.)
"Wake up, wake up you sleepy head,
Get up, get up, get out of bed..."

The door opens. Harry steps out, staring at her.

HARRY
Why are you singing that?

AMY
It's pretty.

HARRY
Why that song?

AMY
What's the matter, Harry?

HARRY
Someone else was singing that
song today.

AMY
A girl?

HARRY
Yes.

AMY
(playfully)
Now, I'M jealous. Who is she?

HARRY
I don't know her...I...it's
something else.

AMY
You never told me where you work,
Harry.

(CONTINUED)

47 CONTINUED: 47

HARRY
Different places. Different jobs.
I'm a musician. A free lance musician.

AMY
Do you live alone, Harry?

HARRY
Why are you asking me questions all of a sudden?

AMY
It's your birthday...I want to know about you.

HARRY
Yes, I live alone, but I don't want to answer any more questions!

He moves to to the kitchenette; we can feel that he doesn't want to stay here anymore.

HARRY
Your rent is due this week.

She doesn't answer.

Here.

He takes out some cash and puts it on a saucer on the shelf.

Food money, too.

She doesn't answer.

I have to go now.

He starts to go, then stops and looks at her. She seems very pale, very vulnerable, very delicate.

You never used to ask me questions.

AMY
I was happy you came tonight, Harry.
My toes were dancing under the covers.
But I don't think I'm going to wait for you anymore.

Harry looks at her; and then leaves.

(CONTINUED)

47 CONTINUED: 47

Her big eyes follow at the spot where he stood for a while, and then she lies back down on the bed.

CUT TO:

48 INT. HARRY'S SMALL LIVING ROOM - NIGHT 48

The single room is dominated by a large homemade loud-speaker, a single speaker as in the old Hi Fi days. We HEAR a Jazz record, old, but well-preserved.

THE VIEW ALTERS and reveals Harry seated on a straight-back wooden chair in the center of his Living Room, holding a saxophone, and furiously playing along with the recording.

The sax solo finishes, to great applause from the live audience, and a sweating, winded Harry closes his eyes and takes it for himself.

FADE OUT:

FADE IN:

49 EXT. HARRY'S BUILDING - DAY 49

A construction crew has begun work on the demolition of an abandoned row of Victorian buildings. We HEAR sounds of trucks and hammers. Harry exits the building, passes the construction work and sits and waits at the stop for the electric bus.

CUT TO:

5Ø EXT. WAREHOUSE AREA - DAY 5Ø

Harry walks parallel to some railroad tracks in the industrial part of the city. Trucks double park, and there is loading and unloading in progress. Perhaps a train goes by.

Harry steps into the warehouse building, pushes a button, and rises up into the building.

CUT TO:

51 INT. HARRY'S WAREHOUSE OFFICE - DAY 51

Harry rises in an industrial elevator up into the warehouse area. We notice benches with electronic equipment, some cabinets and shelves, a screened-off area. Stanley is lounging around on an old sofa reading a magazine.

(CONTINUED)

51 CONTINUED: 51

HARRY
Good morning.

STANLEY
There's an article about the convention here. Mentions your name.

HARRY
Oh yeah?

STANLEY
You're one of the notables who's going tonight. Did you know that?

Harry has taken his coat off, and moves automatically to a workbench where there are three professional tape recorders lined up in a row. Neatly placed by the recorders is a manila folder. Harry opens it.

HARRY
Yes, I said I would go.

He takes several photographs of Ann and Mark in the park which have been recently developed and printed and examines them.

STANLEY (o.s.)
(reading from the magazine)
"...among those pre-eminent in the field expected are Hal Lipsett, and Harry Caul from San Francisco, Kenneth Sperry will also speak on "Surveillance and the Law..."

Harry looks at the photographs. There are glimpses of the couple.

52 CLOSE SHOT ON HARRY 52

Looking.

STANLEY (o.s.)
"...and also attending will be William P. Moran of Detroit, Michigan."

53 CLOSE ON THE PICTURES 53

Now just a view of the girl, Ann, almost as though she is looking at Harry.

54 CLOSE SHOT ON HARRY 54

Looking at the girl, something intrigues him.

(CONTINUED)

54 CONTINUED: 54

HARRY
Since when is William P. Moran pre-eminent in the field?

STANLEY
Coffee?

Stan walks around to an urn, and pours a cup for Harry.

STANLEY
He's very big in Detroit; he's the man who informed Chrysler that Cadillac was getting rid of its fins.

Harry is still looking at the photograph of Ann. Then he puts it to one side of the bench, up where he can see it and begins to work. We can see from the quickness and simplicity of the way he handles the tape and the recorders that he is an expert with these materials. The fragile tape is threaded with two simple movements. Stanley brings him a steaming cup of coffee. Harry indicates with his eyes that it can be placed on the bench.

Now all the recorders are threaded. Harry adjusts the third instrument, one apparently homemade in the shop.

55 MEDIUM VIEW ON STANLEY 55

He is checking out the microphones that were used on the job.

STANLEY
These microphones are really something else. I bet if I wrote up an article or something we could send it to "Security & Surveillance" magazine, don't you think?

HARRY
(the furthest thing from his mind)
Please don't.

Harry turns on the larger console Ampex. There is a beep, a relay is thrown, and the three smaller recorders are started at once. An oscilloscope on the synchronizer shows a perfect electronic circle.

CUT TO:

56 VIEW ON THE LARGE SPEAKER 56

Obviously made by the same hand that made Harry's speaker at home. We hear hiss and static and then Stanley's voice recorded:

STANLEY (o.s.)
Tuesday, December 2nd, one o'clock.
Unit A.
Tuesday, December 2nd, one o'clock.
Unit B.
Tuesday, December 2nd, one o'clock.
Unit C.

We recognize the voices of the couple, Ann and Mark. They echo as though we are hearing the exact same voice from more than one separate recording played at the same time. Harry manipulates a three pot mixer, diverting the strongest and clearest recording to the Ampex.

ANN (o.s.)
"...Wake up, wake up, you sleepy head, Get up, get up, get out of bed...Live, laugh, love and be happy."

57 CLOSE VIEW ON HARRY 57

Listening.

ANN (o.s.)
You got a quarter?

58 EXT. UNION SQUARE - DAY 58

We see Ann and Mark, the exact footage as in the opening, including the fragmentary glimpses of Harry Caul. As they speak we sense another unspoken level through their conversation, as though their minds are not used to really being free with each other in public, as though their minds are not really concentrating on the specific things they're saying, but on a frightened, unbearable love for one another. It is very subtle, and we might not notice it at first, but as we see the scene repeated, it becomes more evident.

ANN (o.s.)
I don't know what to get him for Christmas. He's already got everything.

(CONTINUED)

58 CONTINUED: 58

MARK (o.s.)
He doesn't need anything...anymore.

ANN (o.s.)
I haven't decided...

The VIEW is blocked and the voice track CUTS OUT.

CUT TO:

59 INT. HARRY'S WAREHOUSE - DAY 59

CLOSE VIEW -- THE BLACK ALTEC A-500 LOUDSPEAKER

We hear the only tape hiss.

60 VIEW ON HARRY 60

He quickly presses the button which stops all the units at once. He rewinds them all in synchronization, and then stops. He turns the control knob to forward, and then tapes advance.

61 CLOSER VIEW -- HIS HAND 61

Turns the first knob, and the second one up. We HEAR the conversation superimposed on itself momentarily.

MARK (o.s.)
He doesn't need anything...anymore.

62 EXT. UNION SQUARE - DAY 62

ANN
I haven't decided...(static) what to get you yet.

MARK
Better start looking.

ANN
Well.
(a moment of sadness passes across her face; then she catches herself and brightens:)
Well, what about me?

MARK
You'll see.

CUT TO:

63 INT. HARRY'S WAREHOUSE OFFICE - DAY 63

HIGH FULL VIEW

Harry sits motionless listening to the large speaker. Stanley sits quietly working on some equipment. White light pours through the windows.

ANN (o.s.)
You're no fun. You're supposed to tease me, give me hints, you know.

MARK (o.s.)
Does it bother you?

ANN (o.s.)
What?

MARK (o.s.)
Walking around in circles.

ANN (o.s.)
Look, that's terrible.

CUT TO:

64 EXT. UNION SQUARE - DAY 64

VIEW -- ON THE DERELICT

Lying on the bench, wearing shoes with no socks.

CUT TO:

65 INT. HARRY'S WAREHOUSE OFFICE - DAY 65

THE LARGE LOUDSPEAKER

MARK (o.s.)
He's not hurting anyone.

ANN (o.s.)
Neither are we...
Oh, God.

Harry stops the recorder; rewinds it a bit, and then plays again.

CUT TO:

66 EXT. UNION SQUARE - DAY 66

CLOSE FOOTAGE

Ann and Mark walking past the derelict.

ANN
Neither are we...
Oh, God.

There is tremendous anxiety on her face as she sighs. Then her attention focuses back on the bum.

ANN
Every time I see one of them,
I always think the same thing...

CUT TO:

67 INT. HARRY'S WAREHOUSE OFFICE - DAY 67

VIEW ON STANLEY

Working.

MARK (o.s.)
What do you think?

STAN
(muttering to himself)
Yeah, what DO you think?

ANN (o.s.)
I think he was somebody's baby
boy, and they loved him...

...and here he is now,
half-dead on a park bench
and where is his mother or
his father or his uncles?
Anyway, that's what I
always think.

MARK (o.s.)
I guess I think of how
when they had a news-
paper strike in New York...
Fifty of them died in one
night.

STANLEY
You getting ready for
lunch?

HARRY
I'll skip lunch.

STANLEY
C'mon, we'll go to Al's
Transbay.

HARRY
I want to get this
done.

STANLEY
What a morbid conversation.

(CONTINUED)

67 CONTINUED: 67

ANN (o.s.)
Just because there were no newspapers?

HARRY
Stanley, I'm trying to work.

MARK (o.s.)
Really, it keeps them ... (OUT)

STANLEY
What are they talking about for Chrissakes!

Harry angrily pushes the stop button; all the recorders stop mid-phrase.

HARRY
Listen, I'm trying to get this done!

STANLEY
So don't get excited.

HARRY
I'm getting fed up.

STANLEY
About what?

HARRY
About YOU, asking me questions all day.

STANLEY
JeSUS!

HARRY
Don't say that.

STANLEY
For Chrissakes!

HARRY
Quit saying that in vain. It bothers me.

STANLEY
What's the matter Harry?

Harry pushes the start button.

(CONTINUED)

67 CONTINUED: 67

MARK (o.s.)
warm...

ANN (o.s.)
That's terrible.

MARK (o.s.)
Who started this conversation, anyhow?

ANN (o.s.)
You did.

MARK (o.s.)
I did not.

ANN (o.s.)
You did too, you just don't remember.
(pause)
Mark, it's all right, we can talk.

MARK (o.s.)
I can't stand this...

ANN (o.s.)
You're going to make me cry.

MARK (o.s.)
I know, honey. I know.

(pause)
Me, too....

HARRY
Your work is getting sloppy. We'd have a better track record if you'd pay more attention to the recording and less to what they were talking about.

STANLEY
I can't see why a few questions about what's going on gets you so out of joint.

HARRY
Because I can't sit here and explain..the personal problems of the client.

STANLEY
Hey, you could fill me in a little bit once in a while.

HARRY
It doesn't have anything to do with me... and...and, even less to do with you.

STANLEY
You always keep me in the dark.

HARRY
What am I running here, Manual Arts High School?

STANLEY
It's just goddam human nature.

Harry stops the recorder once again.

(CONTINUED)

67 CONTINUED: 67

HARRY
There's only one sure-fire rule I've learned in this business... It's...I don't know about human nature, I only know about this business.

STANLEY
I'm going to get some lunch. See you later.

Stan angrily takes his coat and steps into the elevator. Its engine whines a moment, as Harry sits frozen on his chair by the bench. When the elevator stops, Harry takes a breath, swivels around back to the bench, and switches on the recording.

ANN (o.s.)
No...don't.

MARK (o.s.)
Oh God...

CUT TO:

68 EXT. UNION SQUARE - DAY 68

Ann is very moved. Mark has put his arm around her caressing her, touching her neck. She pushes his hand away gently. They are both very, very frightened.

ANN
(seriously)
Take a bite out of your sandwich and pretend I just told you a joke.

Mark moves his hand.

Go on.

He breaks out into laughter.

MARK
Where'd you hear that?

ANN
(laughing)
My secret.

(CONTINUED)

68 CONTINUED: 68

She laughs, but it's false and underlined with pain. As they continue walking, we notice the Mime in the background imitating them. They do not notice.

MARK
How do you feel?

ANN
Oh, you know.

MARK
It's a nice day today; yesterday it was cold and foggy.

ANN
Do you...(CUTS OUT)

CUT TO:

69 INT. HARRY'S WAREHOUSE OFFICE - DAY 69

Harry stops the units, reverses them. Brings up the third pot, goes forward once again.

MARK (o.s.)
...cold and foggy.

ANN (o.s.)
Do you think we can do it?

MARK
(much static)
Later in the week. Sunday maybe.

70 CLOSE VIEW ON HARRY 70

Manipulating a filter. Gradually there is less static.

ANN (o.s.)
Sunday definitely...

MARK (o.s)
...3 o'clock. Room B-7.
Continental Lodge.

CUT TO:

71 EXT. UNION SQUARE - DAY 71

CLOSE VIEW ON ANN

The look of fear comes to her face. She watches the man with the shopping bag, as he walks coolly past them.

ANN
Look. See him? The one with the hearing aid...like...

MARK
No. Where?

ANN
He was following us. He kept following us close.

MARK
It's nothing; don't worry about it.

CUT TO:

72 INT. HARRY'S WAREHOUSE OFFICE - DAY 72

CLOSE VIEW ON HARRY

ANN (o.s.)
"When the red, red robin,
Goes bob, bob, bobbin' along, along..."
(pause)
God, it will be so good to be finished with this.

73 HARRY'S HAND 73

Bringing up another pot; echoed, doubled for a moment, then clearly.

ANN (o.s.)
I love you...

74 FULL VIEW OF THE WAREHOUSE 74

We begin to hear on the track the bongo drums.

MARK (o.s.)
We're spending too much time here.

(CONTINUED)

74 CONTINUED: 74

ANN (o.s.)
Stay a little longer.

The drums become louder and louder until we can barely hear them.

MARK (o.s.)
He'd...he'd... (loud drums) ...chance

75 VIEW ON THE BENCH 75

The three symmetrical recorders all stop. They reverse.

76 CLOSE VIEW ON HARRY 76

This was the section he lost.

77 HARRY'S HAND 77

Brings up a second pot. Then pushes the start button.

78 VIEW ON THE TAPE RECORDERS 78

Moving forward.

MARK (o.s.)
He'd...he'd...(the bongo drums distort the few words)...chance.

79 CLOSE ON HARRY 79

Rewinding the tape once again.

80 HARRY'S HANDS 80

He reaches for a little box; something unimpressive, and obviously homemade. A filter of some sort. He connects it to the recorder with the distorted track with alligator clips.

He pushes the forward button, for that one recorder alone.

CUT TO:

81 EXT. UNION SQUARE - DAY 81

Ann and Mark walking by the bongo players. They are speaking, although we hear no words. The sound has

(CONTINUED)

81 CONTINUED: 81

a strange, compressed quality. Each tap of the drums more like an electronic sound. Mark is talking and then one phrase comes through.

MARK (o.s.)
(distorted)
...kill us.

CUT TO:

82 INT. THE WAREHOUSE 82

CLOSE ON HARRY

He hears the word. Stops the recorder. He takes a look at the bench without doing anything. Then quickly he moves.

83 HARRY'S HANDS 83

Disconnect the home-made filter. He pushes it to one side of the bench, and reconnects the recorder as it was.

84 FULL VIEW ON THE WAREHOUSE 84

The tapes are backed up to the point where he had stopped.

ANN (o.s.)
Stay a little longer.

The bongo drums are still loud, obscuring the dialogue now.

MARK (o.s.)
...he'd...(cuts out)...chance.

ANN (o.s.)
(coming out of the Bongo noise)
You know he records the telephones.

85 CLOSE VIEW ON HARRY 85

Listening to the track.

MARK (o.s)
We'd better get back, it's almost two.

CUT TO:

86 VIEW ON THE BENCH 86

The three symmetrical recorders all turning.

ANN (o.s.)
Please don't go back there, please not until...

MARK (o.s.)
Alright, I won't.

CUT TO:

87 EXT. UNION SQUARE - DAY 87

Ann and Mark walk silently for a moment; not looking at each other, their hands at their sides, not touching. In the distant background, we notice the "Mirror Co." van parked across the street.

MARK
You go...I'll stay here awhile.

ANN
Goodbye...wait, you have something on your eye.

She leans toward him, about to brush something away from his eye.

ANN
(whispered)
You really don't, but I want to kiss you.

She uses this chance to kiss him quickly; then turns, and rushes away.

CUT TO:

88 INT. HARRY'S WAREHOUSE OFFICE - DAY 88

FULL VIEW

Harry gets up from his chair, and pushes a button, throwing the entire apparatus into REWIND.

89 CLOSE VIEW ON THE AMPEX 89

Spinning, rewinding itself.

CUT TO:

90 CLOSE VIEW ON HARRY 90

Watching the tape. Then he glances up.

91 HARRY'S VIEW 91

The photograph of Mark and Ann.

DISSOLVE:

92 EXT. TELEPHONE BOOTH - DAY 92

We see Harry from outside the booth.

HARRY
Extension 746.

OPERATOR (o.s.)
One moment.

MALE SECRETARY (o.s.)
The Director's office.

HARRY
Yes, please, this is Mr. Caul.

Harry glances outside. People pass, no one noticing him. He holds a blue vinyl pouch in his hands.

MALE SECRETARY (o.s.)
I'm sorry, he's in a conference right now.

HARRY
I have the material and I'm calling for an appointment.

MALE SECRETARY (o.s.)
We'll call you back later in the afternoon. May I have your number?

HARRY
This is a pay booth. I don't have a telephone.

MALE SECRETARY (o.s.)
Hold on.
(click)

Harry waits. More people pass him.

MALE SECRETARY (o.s.)
Yes. 2:30 this afternoon.

(CONTINUED)

92 CONTINUED: 92

HARRY
2:30 this afternoon, good. Payment in full.

MALE SECRETARY (o.s.)
Whatever was arranged.

Harry hangs up and exits the booth.

CUT TO:

93 INT. LAWYER'S OFFICE (MC NAUGHT) - DAY 93

CLOSE VIEW

A document, in amateur legal terms, giving Harry the right to represent the tenants of 700 Laguna.

MC NAUGHT (o.s.)
The plumbing again, water in the basement...the electrical system.

94 OVER MC NAUGHT TO HARRY 94

MC NAUGHT
...everything but the heat.

HARRY
That's on the next page.

MC NAUGHT
(looking)
...So it is.
Well, what do you want me to do?

HARRY
What will it cost to fix the basement?

MC NAUGHT
We've been through this before.

HARRY
I know.

MC NAUGHT
I recommended we fix the basement last year. I think the bid came in around thirty five hundred dollars.

HARRY
Why don't we just have it pumped?

(CONTINUED)

94 CONTINUED: 94

MC NAUGHT
But the next time it rains, Harry...

HARRY
They're tearing half the neighborhood down. If I can just hold out a little longer the city will buy the building.

MC NAUGHT
And what are you going to tell the tenants' committee?

HARRY
How about...the landlord says positive action will be taken.

MC NAUGHT
Sooner or later they're going to find out the landlord is you. Then what?

HARRY
Then I'll move.
(pause)
They actually gave me birthday presents. Next thing I know they'll make me Chairman of the block party committee.

Mc Naught folds the document, smiling to himself. Harry rises as though to go when Mc Naught pushes two unopened letters toward him.

MC NAUGHT
One second, Harry. I have a little surprise for you.

Harry looks at the letters.

MC NAUGHT
They're from your niece. Also, she's called here several times.

HARRY
(continuing to leave)
I'll call her today.

MC NAUGHT
Don't you want your surprise?

Mc Naught rises and moves toward his study door.

(CONTINUED)

94 CONTINUED: 94

HARRY
(puzzled)
Is....it here?

Mc Naught opens the door to his study and there is TONY, a thirteen year-old girl, sitting on the couch smoking. She has been crying all day. When she notices the door open, she quickly puts the cigarette away and tries to fan the smoke.

TONY
Hello Uncle Harry.

HARRY
Why didn't...why aren't you in school?

MC NAUGHT
I don't think she wants to talk in front of me.

Mc Naught closes the door, leaving them alone.

CUT TO:

95 INT. MC NAUGHT'S STUDY - DAY 95

TONY
I left school...I ran away.

HARRY
Are you all right?

TONY
I want to die.

HARRY
(pause, then he smiles)
Then you're all right.

He moves to her, and kisses her.

TONY
I can't look at you. Don't look at me.

HARRY
I won't. (pause)
You can tell me what happened. I won't look at you.
(pause)

(CONTINUED)

95 CONTINUED: 95

Seeing that the girl still doesn't want to talk, he rises and turns off the lights.

See? Now no one can look at anyone.

He sits very near her. She turns away from him, very embarrassed, very frightened.

TONY

They took us to a dance at Morgan. That's a boys' school in the Valley. I met a boy named Manuel DiSemoza. He can barely speak English, but he comes from a very good family in South America. Venezuela, I think.

(pause)

I had wine with him...and...we were dancing and stuff...and...we really didn't do anything wrong. Not really, Uncle Harry... Are you shocked?

HARRY

No.

TONY

That's because I haven't told you everything, yet.

HARRY

I think I can guess.

The thought that her uncle can even guess what happened causes a flood of tears and embarassment in the little girl.

CLOSE ON HARRY

Moved by her despair and yet unable to say anything that might comfort her.

TONY

(crying to herself)

Uncle Harry, what will I ever do?

(CONTINUED)

95 CONTINUED: 95

VIEW ON HARRY

HARRY

I know...I think I know what it's like not to want anyone to look at you. Sometimes I even rather would talk on the telephone so that the person I'm talking to can't look at me.

(he looks at her so helpless on the couch, moves a little bit toward her)

Don't cry, Tony...I understand. Once something like that happened to me...really. Once my mother caught me in a room with a cousin... I was even younger than you, and she was my favorite cousin...and we were in this room. And we weren't doing anything really. Maybe just like you. But my mother was very religious and she practically kicked the door down and screamed at me when she found us, and called me a deviate...and a pervert, and I didn't even know what those words meant. I was so ashamed, I hid under the covers of my bed and wouldn't look out. I could hear my cousin crying and people coming in and out of my room, and so I just stayed under the covers so nobody could see me. Then I heard the door close, and someone came in and sat on the bed...and touched my head. I couldn't see who it was but he talked to me and I knew it was her father...my uncle. He told me not to be ashamed...that what I did was human and that if a thing was human it couldn't be bad. I was so ashamed I kept crying under the blankets, and so he started to explain all those things to me, that a man was made the way he was and a girl the way she was and that the two desired each other...and that I would understand it soon even if my mother still didn't. After a while I came out from the covers and I could look at my uncle. And I wasn't ashamed any more. (pause) Tony? Tony? Can you look at me?

(MORE)

(CONTINUED)

95 CONTINUED: 95

After a moment the little girl looks up at Harry.

You should be proud that you have those feelings. You don't have to be ashamed to go back to school.

A little embarrassed himself, he looks at her, and she looks up at him gratefully.

I'll take you back to the bus terminal and maybe in a week or two I can come up and visit you on the weekend. Maybe I can even meet Manuel DiSemoza.

The little gratefully hugs her uncle.

CUT TO:

96 EXT. FINANCIAL DISTRICT - DAY 96

Harry crosses a busy street in the financial district and moves in the direction of an impressive tall building. He carries the pouch with him.

CUT TO:

97 EXT. FINANCIAL PLAZA - DAY 97

He moves through the new modernistic plaza towards the elevator.

CUT TO:

98 INT. THE BUILDING ELEVATOR - DAY 98

Harry waits in the elevator as it rapidly fills. A uniformed guard supervises. The doors close and it begins its ascent. We can feel his discomfort at being crowded in with so many people. There are eight or nine conversations going on at once, and his sensitive ears are disturbed by the cacophony.

WOMAN
I told her if that's the way she felt...

VIEW ON HARRY

He turns.

ANOTHER WOMAN
Come with me and Biggs to New...

(CONTINUED)

98 CONTINUED: 98

Harry turns once again.

MAN
She's the cutest...

Floor by floor, the people gradually thin, until Harry is alone. He relaxes, relieved at his privacy.

VIEW ON HIS HANDS

Holding the blue pouch.

The light on the elevator now designates "PH", and the elevator doors open.

CUT TO:

99 INT. DIRECTOR'S SUITE, PENTHOUSE - DAY 99

Harry moves into the reception area, obviously the office of the top executive of this corporation. He moves toward an attractive young man, clean cut, who sits behind a desk in front of a spiral staircase. He is typing, and seems to be the receptionist.

HARRY
I have a delivery for the Director.

RECEPTIONIST
Yes. Please leave it here.

HARRY
It's to be delivered by hand, personally, by me.
I have an appointment.

RECEPTIONIST
Are you Mr. Caul?

HARRY
Yes.

The receptionist says something on the intercom, and turns to Harry.

RECEPTIONIST
Someone will be right with you, Mr. Caul.

(CONTINUED)

99 CONTINUED: 99

Harry waits silently on the sofa. The blue vinyl pouch placed on his lap, his hands folded and resting on it.

RECEPTIONIST
Would you care for a drink?

HARRY
No thank you.

RECEPTIONIST
A soft drink?

HARRY
No.

RECEPTIONIST
Or a magazine?

HARRY
Nothing, thank you.

Harry waits. After a moment, another Young Man descends the spiral staircase and moves directly towards Harry with the expression that he knows him, his hand extended. This is MARTIN.

MARTIN
Good afternoon, Mr. Caul. Can I build you a drink?

HARRY
No, thank you.

MARTIN
Why don't you follow me?

Harry rises, holding onto the pouch, and follows Martin up the spiral staircase.

CUT TO:

100 INT. CORRIDORS - DAY 100

Harry follows Martin through a series of turns in the odd cold corridor. Some employees are putting up Christmas trees and beginning to decorate them.

CUT TO:

101 INT. MARTIN'S OFFICE - DAY 101

Martin waits for Harry to enter and follows and closes the door behind them.

NEW VIEW

Martin sits at his desk, looks at Harry.

MARTIN
I made some Christmas cookies. Try one. They're good.

Martin indicates that Harry may be uncomfortable. Harry sits down.

MARTIN
I have your money here, in cash, like you wanted. Those are the tapes?

HARRY
I was supposed to deliver this to the Director personally. That's the way it was arranged.

MARTIN
Yes, I know, but that's impossible right now. He told me to pay you and collect the tapes.

HARRY
I can wait.

MARTIN
He's out of town...out of the country in fact. Won't be back until tomorrow afternoon, but your payment's been...

Harry rises in the middle of a sentence and picks up the blue pouch.

HARRY
Those were my instructions...

Martin is standing now directly in Harry's way to retrieve the tapes.

MARTIN
Look, Mr. Caul, why get involved in this. Those tapes are dangerous.

(CONTINUED)

101 CONTINUED: 101

CLOSE ON HARRY

Looks at him, reaches, takes the tapes and leaves.

CUT TO:

102 INT. THE CORRIDOR - DAY 102

Harry moves through the corridor, followed a few paces behind by Martin. As he continues, a door opens and out steps Mark, the young man of the recorded conversation, dressed immaculately in the same manner of the other young men who work here. Harry is almost stunned, coming face to face with the subject of his work.

ANN (o.s.)
Please don't go back there, please, not until...

CLOSE ON HARRY

Almost eager to talk to him, to tell him.

MARK (o.s.)
Alright, I won't.

VIEW ON MARK

He glances up at Harry, not recognizing him, giving him the most cursory attention. Martin watches, from a distance.

CUT TO:

103 EXT. UNION SQUARE - DAY 103

REPEATED FOOTAGE

Ann and Mark in their perpetual walk around the quad.

ANN
Look. See him? The one with the hearing aid...like...

MARK
No. Where?

ANN
He was following us. He kept following us close.

(CONTINUED)

103 CONTINUED: 103

She touches his arm and squeezes it.

CUT TO:

104 EXT. AMY'S BUILDING - DAY 104

Harry hurries along the courtyard of Amy's building. Enters.

CUT TO:

105 INT. AMY'S HALLWAY - DAY 105

Harry makes no attempt to be quiet.

ANN (o.s.)
"When the red, red robin,
Goes bob, bob, bobbin' along...
along..."

Harry takes out a key, quite nervous and opens the door.

CUT TO:

106 INT. AMY'S ROOM - DAY 106

ANN (o.s.)
I love you.

HARRY
Amy?

The room is empty. The sheets are off the bed, with the bare mattress folded back over on itself.

MARK (o.s.)
We're spending too much time here.

ANN (o.s.)
Stay a little longer.

We HEAR the sound of the bongo drums on the track.

CLOSE ON HARRY

Looking around the room.

(CONTINUED)

106 CONTINUED: 106

MARK (o.s.)
He'd...(distorted)...chance...

The room is bare and messy, anything personal has been taken. The telephone sits on a little end-table.

ANN (o.s.)
You know he records the telephones.

MEDIUM VIEW

Harry moves through the room, holding the pouch.

MARK (o.s.)
We'd better get back, it's almost two.

Harry moves to the kitchenette; looks up to the cabinet.

MARK (o.s.)
Alright. I won't.

HARRY'S VIEW

He opens the kitchenette cabinet. The saucer is there, still covered with bills, unmoved from where he left them.

MARK (o.s.)
You go...I'll stay here awhile.

FULL VIEW

Harry stands in the empty room, stripped of anything personal. He still holds the pouch.

ANN (o.s.)
Goodbye...wait, you have something on your eye.

CUT TO:

107 EXT. UNION SQUARE - DAY 107

Ann leans forward and steals a kiss.

ANN
You really don't, but I want to kiss you.

She starts to leave.

CUT TO:

108 INT. AMY'S ROOM - DAY 108

FULL VIEW

Of Harry standing in the empty room. We hear only tape hiss and static.

FADE OUT:

FADE IN:

109 INT. THE ST. FRANCIS HOTEL - NIGHT 109

Harry passes through crowds, moving towards the large Convention room. He passes through a mirrored hall-way. The crowds are mainly male, in suits with white convention cards above the vest pocket. Recorded music fills the air with an occasional interruption on the loudspeaker announcing a call for this or that person. Often the names hailed imply that the man is a police-man or a sheriff, or some law-enforcement person.

CUT TO:

110 MOVING VIEW ON HARRY 110

He makes his way toward the reception area of the convention when something he notices disturbs him.

111 HARRY'S VIEW 111

In the crowds of the hotel lobby is the young man with whom he had just dealt at the financial building, Martin. He is fairly far away from Harry, his attention apparently somewhere else, but we have the unmistakable impression that he is following Harry.

112 VIEW ON HARRY 112

Moves quickly through a crowd toward the main entrance of the convention. He stops and looks.

CLOSE ON HARRY

Scanning the room.

HARRY'S VIEW

The young man is no longer there. Harry turns to some pretty hostesses with clipboards of alphabetized names standing by the rows of white name cards. Harry tells one his name, she checks it off, and smilingly pins

(CONTINUED)

112 CONTINUED: 112

a namecard to his suit. Harry moves to the Guard standing by the entrance of the convention room, hesitates, gives one last glance to the area where he had seen the young man, and then enters.

CUT TO:

113 INT. ST. FRANCIS HOTEL CONVENTION ROOM - NIGHT 113

HARRY'S VIEW

Well lit, broken into sections by lettered aisles made up of various booths of exhibitions. Occasionally, we'll catch a sign: "Detector..." "Counter-measure.." "Security...", "Enforcement...". Men are milling around with drinks in their hands, many are huddled around a particular booth. There are a lot of girls in cute outfits pretty and not-so-pretty, walking around, minding the booths, giving demonstrations and flirting with the men.

114 MOVING VIEW ON HARRY 114

Slowly he steps into the room. He is still distracted by the notion that he is being followed. But as he moves deeper in the room, an expression of self-imposed modesty comes over him as through he's embarrassed at the possibility of someone coming up and asking for his autograph.

115 MOVING VIEW 115

On the card on his vest: "Harry Caul".

116 MOVING VIEW ON HARRY 116

Working his way deeper into the exhibition. At one booth he passes, some men are gathered around a thin, enthusiastic man holding out a black box, the components of which are spread out on the table before him.

MAN

The L-T 500 is basically a miniature RF oscillator capable of being activated and modulated by any DC source containing an AC component...

CUT TO:

117 VIEW ON HARRY 117

Giving half-attention to this. Basically scanning through the convention room.

MAN (o.s.)
Such sources can be found in a private telephone or intercom...

118 HARRY'S VIEW 118

We can notice across the convention room the young man entering into the hall, apparently having gotten by the guard.

119 VIEW ON HARRY 119

He turns quickly, moves, moving past another counter, where a sign keeps flashing: NEW, NEW NEW! AT LAST, AT LAST, AT LAST! MINIATURE BATTERY CONTACT AMP.

As he moves by, a pretty girl hands him a fly sheet. Harry makes a turn into some double doors leading to the auditorium. From the inside of the auditorium it's pretty much the same.

CUT TO:

120 INT. AUDITORIUM - NIGHT 120

The auditorium is about 1/3 full. A man stands at the rostrum, delivering a paper, while illustrative slides are being projected on the large white screen behind him.

SPEAKER
...tailing one automobile with another has always presented many unpredictable problems, especially where the subject is aware, or where metropolitan areas at high speeds were encountered. Slide.

The slide changes: A CAR SPEEDING THROUGH THE CITY.

CUT TO:

121 VIEW ON HARRY 121

He glances around the room to see if he recognizes anyone. He gives only cursory attention to the speaker.

(CONTINUED)

121 CONTINUED: 121

SPEAKER
After extensive research and prolonged field testing, F. E. Electronics... Slide...has developed two transistorized units that may be...

122 HARRY'S VIEW 122

Glancing around the auditorium. Some of the men are rapt with attention; others glancing through the circulars they have collected in the plastic convention bags; some are with their wives; one or two are sleeping.

SPEAKER (o.s.)
...affixed to the subject's automobile.
Slide.

123 VIEW ON THE SCREEN 123

A blue box (close up) with several wires terminating out of it into alligator clips.

SPEAKER (o.s.)
...and will transmit a pulsating tone signal which is highly detectable under most conditions...Slide...of electrical...

The slide changes to: A DIAGRAM ILLUSTRATING THE TYPES OF INTERFERENCE THE BOX IS IMMUNE TO.

SPEAKER (o.s.)
...traffic, and mechanical noises.
Slide.

124 VIEW ON THE AISLE 124

Paul Meyers hurries up the aisle to greet Harry. He is very nattily dressed.

PAUL
Harry, Harry, Harry.

HARRY
That's a beautiful suit.

PAUL
You like it? It's French. You know, Millard is here.

(CONTINUED)

124 CONTINUED: 124

HARRY
Really?

PAUL
Yeah, he brought his wife.

HARRY
Same wife he brought two years ago?

PAUL
Same wife. C'mon, let's go where we can get a drink and talk.

They move up the aisle to the exit sign.

SPEAKER (o.s.)
(continuing)
The TA-3Ø may be installed and concealed under the dash in a matter of seconds requiring no knowledge or skill in electronics, and fits with the existing plugs and sockets... Slide.

125 VIEW ON THE SCREEN 125

The slide shows a pretty woman, with skirts high, installing the blue box under the dash.

CUT TO:

126 INT. MAIN CONVENTION ROOM - DAY 126

Harry and Paul enter the main room. Harry quickly scans to see if the young man, Martin, is still there. Paul is rattling on.

PAUL
I told Millard maybe we'd have a little get together later on. I already picked up some booze, potato chips, you know, bean dip. Figured we'd find some bimbos and make a party over at your warehouse. You don't mind, do you, Harry?

Harry is distracted, scanning room for Martin.

HARRY
It's all right.

(CONTINUED)

126 CONTINUED: 126

PAUL
I mean if you minded, maybe we'd go rent a suite in the hotel or something, but I figured that's like burning money.

HARRY
I don't mind.

PAUL
Great. C'mon, there's someone over here you ought to meet.

Paul leads Harry over to the booth designated: "BOOTH #34--WILLIAM P. MORAN & ASSOCIATES." A stringy, curly-haired man, WILLIAM MORAN, stands talking to some conventioneers crowded around his booth. A tall, pretty girl in a yellow satin outfit hands out flyers.

PAUL
Willie, ole buddy, this is Harry Caul. Willie Moran.

MORAN
Heard a lot about you, Harry.

PAUL
Willie just moved out from Detroit. He's the fella who let Chrysler know that Cadillac was discontinuing its fins.

HARRY
I heard.

MORAN
Harry Caul. You're a tough man to get in touch with. I've been wanting to meet you for a long time.

PAUL
Can you take five?

MORAN
(indicating the clock around the booth)
In a minute, fellas. 'Scuse me.
(to the girl)
Honey, show-time.

(CONTINUED)

126 CONTINUED: 126

Her face is smooth and perfect with make-up, like a model. She jumps up from the needlepoint that she tries to do in between customers and picks up a velvet pillow upon which is a bright red telephone.

MORAN (o.s.)
What we have here is the Moran S-15 Harmonica Tap. This electronic marvel can be installed in a matter of two minutes.

The girl, MEREDITH, lowers the telephone on the pillow and Moran quickly slips the tap on it.

MORAN
It has its own Nickel-Cadmium power source, so it can't be detected on the line. Once installed, it can be called from any telephone. Karachi, Singapore even Moscow, fellas.

127 VIEW ON HARRY 127

Preoccupied, is impatient with all this.

MORAN (o.s.)
...just dial the target's telephone number...

CUT TO:

128 VIEW ON MEREDITH 128

With a tired, cupie doll smile as she goes through the demonstration. She notices Harry.

MEREDITH
You in a grump, honey?

MORAN
...pause before the last digit, blow the harmonica tone into the phone...
(he does so)

HARRY
(shaking his head)
Nothing...
(he smiles to her for her concern)

(CONTINUED)

128 CONTINUED: 128

MEDIUM VIEW

MORAN
The phone will not ring in the
target's house! Instead, it will
turn the receiver into a room
microphone, enabling surveillance
to take place.

Meredith winks at Harry.

MORAN
(catching her attention)
Sweetie.
Now, ladies and gentlemen, by way of
a demonstration, we've installed one
of these units in my own house. I
will now dial the number.

Meredith breaks away from her flirtatious concern with Harry to lower the pillow with the phone, so Moran can dial a number. She does it like some funky assistant in a harmonica act, or a stewardess demonstrating oxygen equipment. Moran dials the number, and then blows the harmonica into it.

We hear some tones and clicks.

MORAN
You will take note the phone does
not ring!

Now coming over a loudspeaker so all can hear:

MALE
Can we get away?

WOMAN'S VOICE
I don't know, maybe I can

MALE VOICE
Where's your husband?

WOMAN'S VOICE
He's out, at a convention.

There is a little laughter.

MALE VOICE
When will he be back?

(CONTINUED)

128 CONTINUED: 128

WOMAN
Not until late.

Now we hear hard breathing, passionate breathing simulating love-making. Now more people are laughing.

MORAN
Just a little April Fool. A joke, fellas, but it indicates the possibilities with the Moran S-15.

The demonstration is over, variuos of the crowd pick up fly sheets and examine the unit. Moran returns to Paul and Harry.

PAUL
It's a good item.

MORAN
Yead, good for the catalogue suckers.

He pulls a plastic ball-point pen with his ad printed on it and slips it into their vest pockets.

Here, have a free pen.

PAUL
Rather have a drink.

MORAN
On me. C'mon, let's go get drunk and swap trade secrets, Harry.
(he notices the booth is unminded)
One minute, where is that guy?
Oh Stan, Stan, mind the booth, will you?

Moving over from another part of the hall is Stanley, Harry's former assistant. He wears a nice jacket with the William P. Moran & Associates emblem. He stops when he sees Harry.

STANLEY
Hiya Harry.

MORAN
You two used to work together, didn't you.

(CONTINUED)

128 CONTINUED: 128

HARRY
(understanding)
Yeah.

Moran starts to lead Paul and Harry across the room toward the bar. It's clear that Harry's attention is still focused on his former assistant.

MORAN
Look over there. You see that sonofabitch ELCO Electronics? He's got a new voice actuator that's a copy of mine. Real annoying.

PAUL
Lotsa nice ladies here tonight. What about the pastry in the yellow tights? She come across?

MORAN
Forget it, she's a part-time Nun. I already tried. But we'll pick something up.

Harry hangs back from the fellows going to the bar.

PAUL
Harry? Where you going?

HARRY
I want to talk to Stanley...

He disappears quickly back into the crowd.

PAUL
(calling after him)
We'll meet you later by the Chrome-Dome exhibit.

Harry circles back to the Moran booth. He steps alongside of Stanley.

HARRY
Since when you working for Moran, Stanley?

STANLEY
Since yesterday.

(CONTINUED)

128 CONTINUED: 128

HARRY
That wasn't serious, Stanley, that was a stupid argument.

STANLEY
That wasn't it. I just figured it was about time I move up.

HARRY
You know I...I don't want you telling him about my stuff. It's not ethical.

STANLEY
There isn't all that much that you ever let me in on, Harry. Maybe that's the problem.

HARRY
Stanley. I can take you along faster; I'll show you some of the stuff.

STANLEY
You'll never show me anything; you're going to keep it all to yourself.

HARRY
No, really. Stanley, listen. Don't do this to me now. Wait a while, will you. Think about it.

Harry moves a little closer to Stanley and speaks confidentially.

HARRY
Some guy has been watching me, following me.

STANLEY
Who?

HARRY
I don't know. Someone connected with the assignment last week. I don't know what it's about. I don't like it.

STANLEY
Harry. Harry, you can count on me, you know that.

HARRY
Thank you, Stanley.

(CONTINUED)

128 CONTINUED: 128

Then Harry looks down at a piece of Moran's equipment that he has been mindlessly fingering.

HARRY
Junk.

Harry moves from the booth past another exhibit. Instinctively he feels very uncomfortable when he knows he's being watched. He picks up a piece of equipment, while looking around the room. The man attending the booth jumps up from a chair in which he has been dozing.

MAN
That's your automatic recorder actuator. It undetectably starts a recorder when the phone is lifted and stops it when the receiver is put back.

HARRY
What? Oh...Hmmm hmmm.

The man sleepily leans on the table toward Harry.

MAN
It's real nice, you know. Not your old-fashioned voice actuator, you know, always starting the recorder when no one was talking, or shutting it off in the middle of an important conversation.

He yawns, and pauses while Harry looks it over.

HARRY
Is this anything like the Moran actuator?

MORAN
The Moran E-27 is a copy. I won't let him even smell my equipment anymore. You in Surveillance?

HARRY
Yeah.

MAN
Law Enforcement or Private Operator?

(CONTINUED)

128 CONTINUED: 128

HARRY
Private.

MAN
Mind if I take your name and
address for our mailing list?
(notices Harry's name card)
Harry Caul. Harry Caul? Gee, it's a
great pleasure (extending his warm
hand).
I didn't recognize you.
Say I wonder if you'd take the Model 5-10A
free of charge, just to test it, you know
say in return for letting us print in our
flyer that you use it.

HARRY
(wanting to get away)
Thanks, but I build all my own
equipment.

MAN
But Harry...

CUT TO:

129 INT. THE CONVENTION HALL - NIGHT 129

CLOSE SHOT

A large, spherical mirror reflecting and distorting
fragments of the convention.

MAN'S VOICE (o.s.)
Introducing the attractive, unob-
trusive solution to the surveillance
problem: "Chrome Dome..."

130 PANNING VIEW VIDEO IMAGE 130

The entire Convention area.

MAN (o.s.)
...an exclusive static capsule
designed to observe without intimi-
dation, hidden with the stationary
environmentally protected capsule...

CUT TO:

131 CLOSE SHOT 131

The Dome

MAN (o.s.)
...beautifully designed to represent an imaginative lighting fixture, the Chrome Dome is hinged...

A hand comes down into view and pulls down the Chrome Dome revealing a rotating television camera.

MAN (o.s)
...to permit camera service access.

132 VIDEO IMAGE 132

The scanning camera picks up images of the familiar people of the convention. We see Moran doing the sales pitch. We catch a fragment of Stanley, Paul Meyers putting the make on Meredith, scanning in general the room and some of the characters we have become familiar with, but not Harry.

CUT TO:

133 INT. CONVENTION BAR - NIGHT 133

Harry is dialing on a pay telephone on a corner wall in the bar. The phone rings, rings again, then a click.

RECORDING
You have reached a disconnected number, please check...

He hangs up, seems very disturbed, and is just about to dial again when he notices something.

134 HARRY'S VIEW 134

Seated at the bar, nursing a beer, is Martin, the young man from the Director's office. He smiles and nods to Harry.

135 VIEW ON HARRY 135

Hangs up the telephone and starts out of the bar area, doing a last minute U-turn, reversing his direction and going up to Martin.

CUT TO:

136 CLOSE ON HARRY 136

Disturbed by someone in his business life finding or tracking him here.

HARRY
What are you doing here?

MARTIN
Relax, I'm just a messenger.
Can I buy you a drink, Mr. Caul?

HARRY
You were following me.

MARTIN
Not at all. I was looking for you, Mr. Caul.

HARRY
How did you know I was here?

MARTIN
This is a convention of wire-tappers, isn't it?
Oh, beg your pardon, surveillance and security technicians.
No big guess to find you here.

HARRY
What's the message?

MARTIN
Bring the tapes on Sunday. One o'clock.
The building will be empty, but the guard will let you in.

HARRY
I told you I'll only...

MARTIN
He'll be there, Mr. Caul. Go right to his office...you know where it is.
He'll accept the tapes, in person.

Harry nods and starts out of the bar.

MARTIN
Are the tapes interesting, Mr. Caul?

He looks at Harry.

HARRY
They're excellent.

(CONTINUED)

136 CONTINUED: 136

Harry continues out into the convention area.

CUT TO:

137 INT. CONVENTION AREA - NIGHT 137

Suddenly, an excited Paul Meyers grabs Harry by the arm.

PAUL
Harry, Jesus Christ, come on over to Moran's booth. Crazy Willie threw a bug in the ladies' room. It's hilarious.

He hustles Harry over to the booth where Moran, a couple of other enforcement people, including a husky unpleasant looking man from the mid-West, MILLARD, are all huddled excitedly around a loudspeaker.

PAUL
Hey, here's Harry.

They turn their heads, saying "Shhhhhhh." Some women's voices can be heard echoing around from the hard walls of the ladies' room.

WOMAN'S VOICE
(coming from a speaker)
...first three minutes he says are you going to ball me, or not? Here? I said. Here, in the parking lot. Anywhere, he said.

PAUL
There's this crazy broad in there.

WOMAN'S VOICE
I said I'm not going to ball you in the first three minutes anywhere. I wouldn't ball Paul Newman in the first three minutes!

MILLARD
We've got Stanley stationed at the ladies' john to see who she is.

PAUL
You remember Millard, Harry.

(CONTINUED)

137 CONTINUED: 137

HARRY
How are you Millard? How's your wife; where is she?

MILLARD
Powdering her nose.

Moran breaks into a private laugh.

MORAN
Oh my God. What if it's HER in the ladies' room?

Millard doesn't seem to appreciate his humor. Moran stifles his laugh.

MILLARD
That wasn't funny.

PAUL
He was only joking.

MORAN
(half to himself)
Wire-tapping can be dangerous.

Some of the other men turn around and say "Shhhhhhh" so that they can hear the loudspeaker.

138 ANGLE ON STANLEY 138

Standing by the ladies' room. An older and unattractive woman leaves. He quickly pulls out his walkie-talkie.

STANLEY
I hope for all our sakes that you're still picking up a conversation.

WALKIE-TALKIE
Stay put, Stanley, they're still talking.

STANLEY
Thank God.

CUT TO:

139 ANGLE ON THE BOOTH 139

WOMAN'S VOICE
This thing's closing up in half an hour. You got a date yet?

FIRST WOMAN
I've had five offers, but they're about as stimulating as a sack of grapefruit.

SECOND WOMAN
What do you expect? They're cops. I'll see you later.

Moran excitedly snatches the walkie-talkie away and whispers into it like a CIA agent.

MORAN
(into walkie-talkie)
Stand by, stand by, target's coming out. Stand by to verify target's identity.

140 VIEW ON STANLEY 140

Standing conspicuously by the ladies' room door.

STANLEY
Ten-four, ten-four.

He puts the walkie-talkie away, and waits a moment. Then the door swings open and out steps Meredith, the convention girl from Moran's booth. She notices Stanley.

MEREDITH
(innocently)
Hiya Honey. Peeking into the ladies' room again?

She's changed out of her yellow outfit and carries a small round overnight bag.

141 VIEW ON THE GROUP 141

Meredith makes her way toward them.

PAUL
(to Moran)
That's your idea of a part-time Nun.

(CONTINUED)

141 CONTINUED: 141

MEREDITH
What time do you want me here tomorrow, Mr. Moran?

MORAN
But appropos of nothing, you're surely not leaving, are you honey?

MEREDITH
I told you I was. You said it was all right.

PAUL
When work is done, it's time for play. We're all going to have a party, right Harry?

Harry shrugs. Uneasily he glances over to the side of the convention room, where the ominous young man, Martin, is watching him.

MORAN
A party and you're invited. What do you say?

MEREDITH
Where?

PAUL
Over at Harry's place of business. Right Harry?

HARRY
What? Over at my place?

PAUL
Sure. I asked you before. Don't you remember? You said it was okay.
(out of the side of his mouth)
C'mon, you can't back down now, Harry. I got four hundred girls arriving at your place in half an hour.

Now a pleasant looking woman, very small and petite, very feminine, approaches them. This is LURLEEN, Millard's wife.

MILLARD
Gentlemen, you all know my wife, Lurleen.

(CONTINUED)

141 CONTINUED: 141

They all nod ackowledgements respectively.

MILLARD
(to his wife)
We've been invited to Harry's, for
a little party.

PAUL
Hey, hey, the gang's all here.
We're all going to Harry's for
a party.

MEREDITH
(looking at Harry)
Honey, I go if you go.

142 VIEW ON HARRY 142

Still a little uneasy about Martin watching him.

HARRY
Sure. Yeah, let's get out
of here.

PAUL
Terrific. A hired car awaits
you outside with a liveried chauffeur.

STANLEY
What's liveried mean, anyhow?

CUT TO:

143 EXT. THE ST. FRANCIS PARKING LOT - NIGHT 143

They're all out to the parking lot trying to figure out the best way to put seven adults into Paul's Staff Car (a grey sedan with a code number on the side). Harry keeps glancing over toward the building to see if Martin has followed.

PAUL
All right, Millard can get in
the back with Lurleen and Willie.
No...No..ladies up in the front.
Lurleen, up in the front. Then
Millard in the back. (They all
juggle around, doing so.)

MEREDITH
I thought this was a hired car.

(CONTINUED)

143 CONTINUED: 143

PAUL
Did I say hired? I meant borrowed.

MORAN
From who?

PAUL
From the Vice Squad, who else?
(they laugh)
Okay, Stanley...there you go. And what do you say Harry gets Meredith on his lap.
Everyone A-OK?

The staff car pulls out and joins city traffic.

CUT TO:

144 INT. THE CAR - NIGHT 144

Paul is driving, Harry sits on the passenger side with Meredith on his lap, next to Lurleen. He is uncomfortably crowded, and generally depressed.

MEREDITH
Cheer up, Bunkie. I'm Meredith, who are you?

HARRY
I'm Harry.

Some young guys in a souped-up Mustang zip by them.

PAUL
Sons of bitches. Who are those smart-asses?

He guns the staff car.

PAUL
They don't know who they're tangling with.

CUT TO:

145 EXT. THE STAFF CAR - NIGHT 145

The staff car expertly takes a turn, and tails the Mustang for a while.

CUT TO:

146 INT. THE CAR - NIGHT 146

MILLARD
(appreciatively)
Nice, Paul...

Paul skids the car up to the Mustang as it waits for a light.

PAUL
Hiya fellas! What's that, a field car?

147 VIEW ON THE MUSTANG 147

YOUNG DRIVER
What's a field car?

148 VIEW ON THE STAFF CAR 148

PAUL
A field car goes driving through the field, dropping horseshit, making lettuce grow.

CUT TO:

149 EXT. THE STREET - NIGHT 149

LURLEEN
Oh, Millard, make them stop.

MILLARD
Relax, honey, he's the best tail-man in the country.

PAUL
(driving)
Hear that, Meredith?

MEREDITH
(to Harry, disgusted)
Ha, ha.

CUT TO:

150 EXT. THE STREET - NIGHT 150

In an attempt to lose the grey sedan, the Mustang careens around a corner, almost going out of control. Now the two cars descend down a steep hill.

CUT TO:

151 INT. THE STAFF CAR - NIGHT 151

OVER PAUL'S SHOULDER

As he expertly keeps them in view.

152 VIEW ON STANLEY 152

STANLEY
(shouting out enthusiastically)
Hey, Paul. You're Bullitt. Get it, you're Bullitt.

153 VIEW ON PAUL 153

PAUL
Check this. I'm Bullitt! I'm Steve McQueen!

Everyone in the car laughs.

154 CLOSER VIEW 154

On the Mustang's license plates: GVO 587

155 CLOSE VIEW ON PAUL 155

He reaches under the dash and pulls out a mobile telephone receiver.

PAUL
Headquarter One Eleven to Headquarters. Headquarter One Eleven, I'm travelling eastbound on Oak from Masonic. I'd like a rolling 1Ø28, please, on California George Victor Ocean 587.

MILLARD
What are you running a 1Ø28 for?

PAUL
(into phone)
Thanks, fellas.

CUT TO:

156 EXT. THE STREET - NIGHT 156

The Mustang has stopped for another light. Paul screeches to a stop alongside it.

CUT TO:

157 INT. THE CAR - NIGHT 157

MEREDITH
(to Harry)
Jesus, what are we going to do
next? Play in the sandbox?

158 VIEW ON PAUL 158

Across to the kids in the Mustang.

PAUL
Hey, Willie Sanchez, 33654 14th
Street. Asshole!

CUT TO:

159 INT. THE CAR - NIGHT 159

The staff car roars off, giving the Mustang a blast of its SIREN and leaving the kids totally amazed and stalled at the light.

CUT TO:

160 INT. HARRY'S WAREHOUSE - NIGHT 160

The warehouse is dark.

161 VIEW ON THE WORKBENCH--PANNING 161

With the three recorders still laid out; the large black speaker silent and omnipresent.

As the view moves along the bench, we see various examples of Harry's devices.

In the distance, we HEAR the elevator's engine whining and Paul and Meredith singing.

PAUL & MEREDITH (o.s.)
"I'll be out to get you in a taxi,
honey. Better be ready about half
past eight..."
(laughter)

VIEW SETTLES ON THE ELEVATOR

The incandescent-lit elevator rises out of the floor crowded with Paul holding four whiskey bottles; Meredith carrying ice; Stan holding six-packs of beer cans; Millard and Lurleen, Moran holding sack of potato chips.

(CONTINUED)

161 CONTINUED: 161

PAUL & MEREDITH (o.s.)
"Now honey don't be late..."

The elevator arrives. Stanley steps out and turns on the fluorescent fixtures. The little party enters.

MEREDITH
You live in a warehouse?

PAUL
No, he doesn't live here, babe, he works here.

MORAN
The bar is open.
Harry, you got a nice place here.

Harry has wandered over to the window and paranoically glances out one last time. Then he moves automatically to his workbench area and closes the wire mesh cage that separates it and all his devices from the main part of the warehouse.

MEREDITH
Harry is the color of a Christmas tree.

MORAN
What's the matter? Got personal problems?

MILLARD
How about some music, fellas?
Stanley?

MORAN
When a guy excuses himself every ten minutes to make a phone call, cherchez la femme, I always say.

Moran puts a drink in Harry's hand. Stan has put a fast jazz record on.

MEREDITH
Something slow.

STANLEY
Gotcha.

He proceeds to change the record.

(CONTINUED)

161 CONTINUED: 161

MORAN
I was re-reading "Dear Abby" the other day and I was reading this letter from a fella called "Lonely and Anonymous." I think it was Harry.
(he breaks in to laughter)

Stanley has changed the record to a nice, slow fox-trot.

MORAN
No, I'm kidding. Let me tell you something about Harry Caul. Harry, I know you heard it a thousand times, but let me say it again. Harry is the best, bar none.
(raising his glass)
Harry Caul, the best bugger on the West Coast.
(he drinks)

MILLARD
And who's the best on the East Coast?

MORAN
Me. I'll drink to that, too!

They all laugh and drink.

PAUL
(taking Meredith's hand)
Are you free for this dance?

MEREDITH
I'll dance, but I'm not free.

Paul and Meredith start to dance around the warehouse, still holding their drinks.

MORAN
Hey, you know it's funny we never bumped into you in New York.

HARRY
Why is that funny?

MORAN
Well, being in the same business in the same city, I figured we would have run into each other.

(CONTINUED)

161 CONTINUED: 161

STANLEY
I didn't know you came from New York, Harry.

MORAN
Harry was famous in New York. You know one I could never figure out.

HARRY
One what?

MORAN
The welfare fund back in '68.

HARRY
Where'd you hear about that?

MORAN
Everyone in the biz heard about it. No one knows how you did it though.

STANLEY
Hey, Paul, what about those phone calls you were gonna make?

PAUL
Right away, Stan, right away.

He moves to the phone and starts to take out a book. Meredith laughingly leaves him and moves to Harry while Paul, in the background, starts to make phone calls. She takes him by the hand.

MEREDITH
C'mon Harry, ten cents a dance.

Millard is taking the brochures from the Convention out of the plastic bag and explaining them to his wife, Lurleen, who seems bored and sips on a drink.

MILLARD
You can use it in an ordinary .38 calibre revolver. It travels down the barrel, spinning, and as it leaves the muzzle it opens into a a pancake-like projectile about the size of a quarter.

Stanley crowds Paul while he makes one of his phone calls.

(CONTINUED)

161 CONTINUED: 161

PAUL
Hiya Veronica? This is Paul. Oh...
Oh, Veronica's in L.A. Well, what's
your name. Verna? Verna, this is
Paul. I'm a friend of Veronica's.
What are your doing?

As Meredith swings in to dance with Harry she bumps her head on a low-hanging fixture.

MEREDITH
Excuse me for the hardness of
my head.

HARRY
You hurt your head?

MEREDITH
Don't worry about my head. It
happens all the time. When I was
a baby I used to love to bang my
head up against the wall, or so I
was told. It's comforting.

Paul hangs up the phone in the background and looks for another number. Then he notices Harry dancing with Meredith and shouts out.

PAUL
(shouting)
Hey, Harry, you hear the one about
the surveillance man's girlfriend.
She wore a see-through blouse.

He breaks into hysterical laughter at this reference to Meredith's blouse.

MEREDITH
Ha, ha.
(intimately to Harry)
I didn't know Paul was a cop. Is he
a detective or something?

HARRY
Special services. The Vice Squad.

MEREDITH
Oh, Christ, that's all I need. A
hot date with the Vice Squad.
(she squeezes against Harry)
Rather be with you, hon.

CUT TO:

162 VIEW OF MILLARD AND LURLEEN 162

MILLARD
...It's lethal up to fifty feet, but it doesn't go through the target, so it doesn't damage any property.
(he looks at his wife)
What do you think, honey?

LURLEEN
It's cold in here.

Moran refills Harry's drink, walking with them as he dances with Meredith.

MORAN
Harry, c'mon, figure this one out. This'll kill you. Two men are going to have a big meeting. It'll be dangerous. One's got an Italian name, so you know what I mean. They're going to talk in the old paisan steam bath, naked.

MEREDITH
I got the whole thing for the Justice Department. Tell me how I did it?

HARRY
(easily)
The transmitter was in the soap.

Stanley breaks into laughter.

STANLEY
In the soap!

But from Moran's disgruntled expression, we realize that's where it was.

MORAN
You read that in my book.

HARRY
I never read your book.

Lurleen slips her Mink coat over her shoulders.

LURLEEN
It's cold in San Francisco.

CUT TO:

163 VIEW ON PAUL 163

On the telephone. Stan is nearby.

PAUL
Hiya, Beth? Paul Meyers. Meyers!

164 VIEW ON MEREDITH AND HARRY 164

Meredith has danced Harry away from Moran.

MEREDITH
Where you from, hon?

HARRY
New York.

MEREDITH
Me too. I used to work for a man who owned a whole chain of hardware stores. First I was a receptionist then I got promoted to a secretary, and then I got promoted to gal-Friday and special assistant to the boss. Then I married him.

He got bit by the stock market and invested all his money in a company called "Galloping Goose" which is an airplane that flies by moving its wings up and down.

HARRY
How'd he do?

MEREDITH
C'mon Harry. When's the last time you spotted an airplane flapping its wings?

Harry laughs.

MEREDITH
(flirtatiously)
You live far from here, honey?

She cuddles close to him and they dance intimately for a while.

HARRY
You still married?

(CONTINUED)

164 CONTINUED: 164

MEREDITH
Probably. Last thing I heard he was trying to scrape enough money together to by a little hardware store. Somehow I ended up unemployed in San Francisco, which is my entire life history up to tonight.

What's the matter, don't you like to talk?

HARRY
No.

Harry holds on to Meredith and they don't speak for a while, but dance intimately. We can hear fragments of the conversations of other people.

MILLARD
...the miniaturization; the circuits are smaller, more efficient; there's no end to it.

MORAN
The end to it is that I'm gonna make a fortune selling the stuff to you and go retire in Rio de Janeiro.

Something is obviously on Harry's mind, something that troubles him. He looks at Meredith.

MEREDITH
What's on your mind?

Harry doesn't respond.

You want to tell me about it, I can tell.

HARRY
Meredith...would you...

MEREDITH.
Would I want, Harry?

Harry doesn't go on.

Go on, Harry, you can ask me.

(CONTINUED)

164 CONTINUED: 164

HARRY
(very quietly, it's difficult for him to talk about personal things)
If you were a girl who waited for someone...
(he hesitates)

MEREDITH
Go on, sweetheart, you can ask me anything.

HARRY
...and you never really knew when he would come to see you. You just lived in a room alone and knew nothing about him. And...if you loved him and were patient with him and still he didn't dare tell you one personal thing about himself.
(pause)
...Even though he may have loved you. Would you...

MEREDITH
Would I?

HARRY
Would you go back to him?

MEREDITH
But how would I know he loves me?

HARRY
You would have no way of knowing.

MEREDITH
Then I wouldn't go back to him.

There is a sudden tap on Harry's shoulder. Paul is behind them.

PAUL
Harry, I mean we're the musketeers. One for all and all for one.

He substitutes himself in Meredith's arms, leaving Harry alone and awkward on the warehouse floor.

Harry wanders back to the chairs where Moran, Stan and Millard and Lurleen are sitting.

(CONTINUED)

164 CONTINUED: 164

MORAN
(boasting)
Twelve years ago I recorded every telephone conversation that the Republican nominee for the Presidency made, all over the country during his campaign, on trains, on planes, everywhere he went.
(he smiles)
He lost.

STANLEY
Harry, tell them about the time you put the bug in the parakeet. No, I'm serious, Harry actually put a microphone in a parakeet.

MORAN
I want to hear about that Welfare Fund back in 1969.

MILLARD
What was that?

MORAN
You must have read about it in the papers. Harry was working for the Attorney General's office.
(quickly pointing his finger at Harry)
Didn't know I knew that, did you, Harry? Anyway, the President of a Local back in the East had this phony welfare fund set up. Talked about it on these fishing trips he went on with his accountants. A private boat. That was the only place they talked about details. And the boat was bug-proof. They wouldn't even start up a conversation of there was another boat on the horizon. Harry recorded the whole thing.

Reference to this case seems to irritate Harry.

MORAN
No one's ever figured out how you did it. Caused a helluva scandal.

PAUL
Why?

(CONTINUED)

164 CONTINUED: 164

MORAN
Three men were murdered because of it. Harry's too modest to tell us how he did it, though.

HARRY
(quietly)
It had nothing to do with me, I mean, I just turned in the tapes.

MORAN
The President thought the Accountant had talked.

HARRY
No one really knows for sure.

MORAN
They found him naked with all his hair on his body shaved, with his hands and feet tied up with a rope, and his head in a different place.

LURLEEN
They killed him?

MEREDITH
This is morbid.

MORAN
C'mon, Harry, it's ancient history. Now, how'd you do it?

HARRY
What they do with the tapes is their own business.

MORAN
That's when I first heard about you. The next thing I knew you moved out of New York.

HARRY
It had nothing to do with me.

MORAN
C'mon, Harry, show and tell. How'd you do it?

PAUL
C'mon, fess up Harry.

(CONTINUED)

164 CONTINUED: 164

HARRY
(quietly)
I pre-rigged the bait box. When they picked up their bait, they picked up my transmitter.

ANN (o.s.)
"Wake up, wake up you sleepy head..."

165 CLOSE ON HARRY 165

Startled.

ANN (o.s.)
"Get up, get up, get out of bed..."

MORAN
What's that?

ANN (o.s.)
"Cheer up, cheer up, the sun is red..."

Harry turns and looks.

166 HARRY'S VIEW 166

Stanley has opened the wire-mesh that protects the workbench area and has turned on the master tape of the recent recording that Harry made.

167 CLOSE VIEW 167

The photograph of Mark and Ann that Harry has put by his bench.

HARRY
Turn it off, Stanley.

ANN (o.s.)
"You got a quarter?"

STANLEY
They ought to hear this. This is the best you've ever done, Harry.

HARRY
Stanley, turn it off!

Stan clicks it off.

STANLEY
Sure, Harry.

(CONTINUED)

167 CONTINUED: 167

Harry looks at him angrily. Meredith has wandered into the area, by some crude, unpainted bookshelves.

MEREDITH
Look, roses!

The bookshelves are filled with odd items, sort of like a prop shelf. There are radios, ashtrays, packs of cigarettes, cigar humidors, vases. She is holding up a bouquet of roses, putting them provocatively by her cleavage.

MEREDITH
Are these for me, Harry? You shouldn't have.

STANLEY
You now got a microphone in your tits!

Moran gives a loud, vulgar laugh.

MORAN
That's the funniest thing I ever saw.

LURLEEN
Millard...

Stanley moves to Meredith, shows her the tiny microphone hidden in one of the artificial flowers.

STANLEY
See...all this stuff; different stuff Harry's used over the years.

He pulls some electronic components out of a pack of cigarettes.

Everything but the Martini olive.

Harry moves to the area and indicates to both Stanley and Meredith that they should come out of the fenced-off area. As they do, he closes the door once again.

MORAN
(blase)
All that stuff's obsolete, of course. We sell that to mail order detectives and nervous husbands.
Right partner? (to Harry)

(CONTINUED)

167 CONTINUED: 167

This annoys Harry.

STANLEY
Ah, but Harry's done a job this week that's gonna make history.
(to Moran)
You'd never figure it out.

MORAN
There's no moment between human beings that I cannot record, and there is no method that I cannot figure out.

PAUL
You couldn't figure out the bait box routine.

MORAN
I knew it all the time. I was puttin' Harry on. It's in my book, smartass.
(to Harry)
Harry knows I could figure any of his things out.

HARRY
Maybe.

STANLEY
Go on, Harry, give him the assignment.

Harry takes out a piece of chalk and draws a square on the blackboard.

HARRY
This is a quad. Here's a quad in the center of the city. There are steps.
(drawing)
Benches all around. It's 12:3Ø which is lunch time for a lot of people who work in the offices nearby. The place is filled with peole talking, walking, having lunch. Two people are constantly walking in circles in and out of the crowds. You don't know whether they'll sit down or not. They feel pretty secure that because they're in a crowd and constantly moving that it's impossible to record them. Yet they're the targets, and the assignment is to get everything they're saying. How would you do it?

(CONTINUED)

167 CONTINUED: 167

MORAN
One system wouldn't do it.

HARRY
Alright.

MILLARD
I could've told you that.

MORAN
It's easy. Plant a bug on them, get to their clothes.

HARRY
There's no way of knowing what they're going to wear.

MORAN
Well, then have someone bump into them, a drunk or something. Slip a pin mike on them.

HARRY
The targets know they've been bugged before. Too risky and obvious for them.

MORAN
(confidently)
Hire a lip reader with binoculars.

HARRY
The client wants THEIR voices, specifically.

MORAN
Why?

HARRY
So he can believe it.

MILLARD
Who are they?

HARRY
A boy and a girl. I don't know.

PAUL
(to Millard)
Shhhhhh.
(to Moran)
Go on, smartass.

(CONTINUED)

167 CONTINUED: 167

MORAN
Must have been en expensive show. Who was so interested?

MILLARD
Was it us?

MEREDITH
Who's us?

MILLARD
The Federal government.

Meredith makes a gesture that she's impressed.

HARRY
No. A private party.

Moran looks at the blackboard.

168 VIEW ON THE BLACKBOARD 168

MORAN
It would take at least four passes.

HARRY
I did it in three.

MORAN
Nice. What did you use?

HARRY
I tracked them with three-stage dimensional microphones of my own design. Then we picked up another twenty percent just tailing them conventionally. Paul did it.

STANLEY
It was a work of art, it really was a work of art.

PAUL
You should have seen it.

This seems to be the one subject which truly excites Harry.

(CONTINUED)

168 CONTINUED: 168

HARRY
(becoming enthusiastic)
These new microphones are like nothing I've ever used before. I almost didn't believe it myself. We were almost over 200 hundred yards away and it was totally readable. I broke in a newsreel cameraman on the mike. It was a beautiful thing to see, really beautiful.

LURLEEN
What did they do?

HARRY
They tracked them cross-hair on the button right on their mouths.

LURLEEN
No. The boy and the girl. What did they do?

HARRY
(almost puzzled why anyone would ask)
I don't know. I don't know. It was beautiful. You should've seen it.

MORAN
Sounds pretty. I'd like to see those mikes.

HARRY
Fat chance.

MORAN
I've been telling you, Harry, that the two of us ought to get together. I said you're the best, didn't I? You and me together, that's the tops. Let me into those file cabinets of yours, those little drawings and those little devices. We'll make a fortune selling stuff to Uncle Sam.

HARRY
I don't want a partner.

MORAN
Harry, I'm pretty good too. I mean give credit where credit is due. I mean abracadabra. How's this?

(CONTINUED)

168 CONTINUED: 168

He takes a small cassette recorder out of his pocket and lays it on the table.

MORAN
I'm number two. I have to try harder!
(he laughs)

He switches on the recorder. There is hiss and static and then:

MEREDITH (o.s.)
Go on, Harry, you can ask me.

HARRY (o.s.)
If you were a girl who waited for someone...

169 CLOSE ON HARRY 169

Slowly he realizes what he's been listening to.

MEREDITH (o.s.)
Go on, sweetheart, you can ask me anything.

HARRY (o.s.)
...and you never knew when he would come to you. You just lived in a room alone...

HARRY (o.s.)
and you knew nothing about him. If you loved him and were patient with him and still he didn't dare tell you one personal thing about himself.
(pause)
Even though he may have loved you. Would you...

MEREDITH
Harry! That's you! That's you and me!

HARRY
Alright...Shut it off.

PAUL
No shit. That's terrific. The bugger got bugged. (he laughs)

HARRY
Alright, we heard it. Shut it off now.

MEREDITH (o.s.)
Would it?

HARRY (o.s.)
Would you come back to him?

(CONTINUED)

169 CONTINUED: 169

Harry reaches over and shuts off the cassette recorder. The others are still laughing. Moran reaches over to the upset Harry and flips out the pen he had given them, unscrewing it revealing the mechanism.

MORAN
The Moran B-27 Mike and Transceiver!

PAUL
Touche, Harry, touche. You were had.

MORAN
C'mon, Harry, just a gag, for Chrissakes! Drink up, will you?

STANLEY
(sincerely)
Willie, Harry doesn't like you to say "Chrissakes."

170 VIEW ON HARRY 170

Embarassed and angry over having these intimate thoughts exposed.

171 HARRY'S VIEW 171

The various members of he party; laughing, mimicking the things Harry said.

172 VIEW ON LURLEEN 172

The laughter wakens her; she looks around, confused. Then she joins in on the laughing.

173 VIEW ON HARRY 173

HARRY
I...I...let's...

PAUL
Harry, what's the matter.

HARRY
I didn't really want you here...
I really...

MORAN
Harry, don't get sore.

(CONTINUED)

173 CONTINUED: 173

HARRY
Please get out!

PAUL
But we're having a party.

HARRY
Just get out and leave me alone.

MILLARD
C'mon, honey.

MORAN
What're you getting so upset over?

STANLEY
C'mon, we'd better go.

Stanley starts to pick up some of the still-full bottles and move to the elevator. Paul helps him.

PAUL
(to Meredith)
Let's go, honey.

Meredith stands there, looking at Harry.

MEREDITH
Harry?

Harry doesn't answer her. The group have awkwardly gathered their stuff, and are ready to descend as soon as Meredith joins them.

PAUL
Meredith...

MEREDITH
I want to stay.

She looks at Harry. He doesn't seem to contradict her. Stanley pushes the button, and the elevator starts down; we HEAR a confused mumble of whispers as they talk about Harry on the way down.

After a moment, Meredith is in the empty warehouse, standing looking at Harry. We HEAR voices fade, and then the sounds of the doors, and then everything is quiet.

(CUT TO)

174 ANGLE ON MEREDITH 174

Meredith moves around the warehouse, quietly picking up the paper cups and potato-chip sacks and the junk left by the party.

HARRY
(quietly)
It was my birthday yesterday.

MEREDITH
(with no expression)
Happy Birthday, Harry.

She continues picking up things, and in a few moments, most of the mess is gone.

She moves to him and a mischievous little smile comes over her face.

MEREDITH
I liked you best when I first saw you. Couldn't you tell?

HARRY
No.

MEREDITH
(moving to him)
What's the matter, Harry?

HARRY
I don't know...I haven't...sometimes I have trouble falling asleep. And I've been nervous.

She looks at him with an easy, but true-felt compassion.

MEREDITH
Harry, Harry, Harry...

HARRY
I dream every night but it's...it's like I'm still awake. Then the next day I don't...I don't feel as though I've slept at all.

MEREDITH
(sincerely)
Harry, Harry...

(CONTINUED)

174 CONTINUED: 174

HARRY
And lately...for the first time almost, I've been lonely.

MEREDITH
It's this God-awful business you're in. It has got to be the crummiest I've ever heard of.

HARRY
I oughta quit.

MEREDITH
Good. Why don't you?

HARRY
I love it...

MEREDITH
But a man with your brain and knowing about, you know, that stuff. You could have been in the Stereo business or the Record business or something really exciting. And important. I knew a guy in the record business in Detroit. And he did far out records. You should have heard them. One was called "Jardin de Eros," Sounds of Lust. It was the filthiest thing I've ever heard in my life. You ever heard one of those records?

HARRY
No, I haven't.

MEREDITH
Well, you're missing something. I can talk openly with you. Well, it comes on and you can hear this sound: Petunk, petunk, petunk. Which is, of course, stereophonic bedsprings. Then this lady...I call her a lady...but she says:
(pause)
Oh, you don't want to hear this.
(she moves a lot closer)
You could do anything, Harry. A man like you.

(CONTINUED)

174 CONTINUED: 174

HARRY
(whispered)
I dream about that tape...

MEREDITH
(whispered)
What?

HARRY
(whispered)
The tape, the tape. It's not
an ordinary conversation...

MEREDITH
(whispered)
What are you talking about?

HARRY
(whispered)
It makes me feel...something...

MEREDITH
(breaking this mood with
full voice)
Forget it, Harry...it's just a trick.

HARRY
What...

MEREDITH
A job. You don't have to FEEL anything
about it. You just have to do it.
That's all honey, don't worry.

She moves to him, and slowly kisses his mouth.

MEREDITH
How in God's creation did an
attractive man like you manage to
stay single.

HARRY
I'm difficult to live with.

MEREDITH
(moving him to the sofa)
Lie down, Harry. I'll rub your back.

Harry moves away, moves to the recorder. Looks at the partially unspooled tape.

(CONTINUED)

174 CONTINUED: 174

MEREDITH
Come back here. I want to show
you a little trick I learned in
Military School.

Slowly Harry lifts his hand, rests it on the switch.

MEREDITH
Are you going to give me trouble
tonight?

He turns on the switch. The spools begin to turn.

ANN (o.s.)
I haven't decided (static) what
to get you yet.

175 CLOSE ON HARRY 175

Listening intently, as though for the first time, he's listening to THEM, and not to his own technology. We can see Meredith standing by the sofa in the distant background.

MARK (o.s.)
Better start looking.

MEREDITH
Harry.

ANN (o.s.)
Well.
(pause)
Well, what about me?

HARRY
(whispered to himself)
Why..why...what is she frightened of?

MARK (o.s.)
You'll see.

MEREDITH
Turn it off.

ANN (o.s.)
You're no fun. You're supposed to
tease me, give me hints, you know.

HARRY
(barely audible)
...give me hints.

(CONTINUED)

175 CONTINUED: 175

MEREDITH
Harry, come here...

MARK (o.s.)
Does it bother you?

ANN (o.s.)
What?

MARK (o.s.)
Walking around in circles.

Slowly, Meredith moves to him.

ANN (o.s.)
Look, that's terrible.

MARK (o.s.)
He's not hurting anyone.

ANN (o.s.)
Neither are we...Oh, God.

Meredith kisses Harry on his neck.

HARRY
(painfully)
Oh, God, listen to the way she
says "Oh, God."

Meredith takes Harry's hand and begins to lead him back to the sofa.

ANN (o.s.)
Everytime I see one of them, I
always think the same thing.

Meredith takes Harry to the sofa, and gently pushes him to lie down.

MARK (o.s.)
What do you think?

176 CLOSE ON HARRY 176

Listening.

ANN (o.s.)
I think he was somebody's baby boy,
and they loved him...

CUT TO:

177 MEDIUM VIEW 177

Harry lying on the sofa. We see only fragments of Meredith as she gently loosens his shoes, and pulls them off, one by one.

ANN (o.s.)
...and here he is now, half-dead on a park-bench, and where is his mother or his father or his uncles.

Meredith walks past him, and out of Frame, leaving this pathetic, derelict view of Harry.

ANN (o.s.)
...anyway, that's what I always think.

MARK (o.s.)
...I guess I think of how when they had a newspaper strike in New York, more of those old drunks died in one night because they didn't have newspapers to cover themselves with.

Harry shudders with cold and fear.

ANN (o.s.)
Just because there were no newspapers?

MEREDITH
Just because there were no newspapers?

She walks by once again, having taken off her dress. Her long, naked legs interrupting our VIEW of Harry, momentarily.

MARK (o.s.)
Really, it keeps them warm.

178 MEDIUM CLOSE VIEW ON HARRY 178

Meredith's white hands come into VIEW, and unbutton his shirt.

ANN (o.s.)
That's terrible.

MARK (o.s.)
Who started this conversation, anyhow?

ANN (o.s.)
You did.

MARK (o.s.)
I did not.

(CONTINUED)

178 CONTINUED: 178

ANN (o.s.)
You did too. You just don't remember.

MEREDITH
(pulling off Harry's shirt)
She started it.

Meredith crosses to the bathroom, wearing a top, but no bottom.

The door closes.

THE VIEW MOVES CLOSER TO HARRY

ANN (o.s.)
Mark...it's all right...we can talk.

MARK (o.s.)
I can't stand this.

HARRY
Listen...

ANN (o.s.)
You're going to make me cry.

HARRY
Listen...

MARK (o.s.)
I know honey. I know.
(pause)
Me too.

ANN (o.s.)
No...don't...

MARK (o.s.)
Oh, God...

HARRY
Oh, God...

ANN (o.s.)
Take a bite out of your sandwich.

The bathroom flushes.

...and pretend I just told you a joke.

Meredith comes back from the bathroom.

(CONTINUED)

178 CONTINUED: 178

MARK (o.s.)
(laughter)
Where'd you hear that?

ANN (o.s.)
My secret.

MEREDITH
They're having more fun than we are.

MARK (o.s.)
How do you feel?

ANN (o.s.)
Oh, you know.

179 MEDIUM VIEW 179

Now a fragment of Meredith moves across Harry, and we know she is unbuttoning his trousers and pulling them off.

ANN (o.s.)
Do you think we can do it?

MARK (o.s.)
Later in the week. Sunday, maybe.

ANN (o.s.)
Sunday, definitely.

MARK (o.s.)
...3 o'clock. Room B-7. Continental Lodge.

Now Meredith carefully folds Harry's trousers, and folds them on the back of a chair. She takes off her own blouse.

ANN (o.s.)
Look. See him? The one with the hearing aid...like...

MARK (o.s.)
No. Where?

ANN (o.s.)
He was following us. He kept following us close.

(CONTINUED)

179 CONTINUED: 179

Meredith's long naked body slips expertly onto the sofa with Harry, and she pulls a make-shift blanket over both of them. Her hand touches Harry's face.

180 CLOSE VIEW ON HARRY 180

Sweating and frightened.

MARK (o.s.)
It's nothing; don't worry about it.

ANN (o.s.)
"When the red, red robin,
Goes bob, bob bobbin' along, along."

MEREDITH
Hey...angel.

She uses the edge of the blanket to wipe the perspiration from his face.

ANN (o.s.)
God, it will be so good to be finished with this.

Meredith moves to him, and sweetly kisses him.

ANN (o.s.)
I love you.

MEREDITH (o.s.)
It's alright, baby.

MARK (o.s.)
We're spending too much time here.

ANN (o.s.)
Stay a little longer.

Meredith kisses his forehead, his eyes, his neck.

MARK (o.s.)
...he'd...chance...

ANN (o.s.)
You know he records the telephones.

MARK (o.s.)
We'd better get back, it's almost two.

HARRY
(whispered)
...kill us...
(pause)
He'd kill them if he had the chance.

HARRY
(painfully)
Oh, what have I done...

(CONTINUED)

180 CONTINUED: 180

ANN (o.s.)
Please don't go back there, not until...

MARK (o.s.)
(after a moment)
Alright. I won't. You go...I'll stay here awhile.

ANN (o.s.)
Goodbye...wait, you have something on your eye (pause) You really don't, but I want to kiss you.

MEREDITH
Shhhh, it's all right.

HARRY
It was true. It was true. Those three men were murdered because of me.

MEREDITH
I know, Harry. I know. I really know. I really do.

HARRY
They have no protection. I can find them wherever they go, and I can HEAR them...

MEREDITH
Shhhh, I forgive you. I forgive you, Harry.
(whispering into his ear)
I forgive you. Shhhhhh.
(she puts her tongue into his ear.)

THE VIEW HAS SLOWLY PANNED

to the large black Altec speaker. We HEAR the hiss and electric hum.

DISSOLVE:

181 INT. THE WAREHOUSE - NIGHT 181

CLOSE VIEW ON HARRY

Asleep, although we can sense his eyes moving quickly under his lids. We HEAR the sounds of the city in the middle of the night: the electric buses, the fog horns. Meredith lies next to him, cuddled, sound asleep.

DISSOLVE:

182 EXT. UNION SQUARE - DAY 182

Mark and Ann in their perpetual walk around Union Square. We HEAR only the sounds of the city at night, continuing. This VIEW of them seems overly-bright, odd. We hear nothing of what they say; and sense only the anxiety and fear that underlines their every expression.

SUPERIMPOSE:

183 INT. THE WAREHOUSE - DAY 183

THE BIG BLACK SPEAKER, in the silent warehouse. Then PAN across to the bench, where we can see the tape on the recorder, still turning, although long off the reel.

DISSOLVE:

184 HARRY ASLEEP 184

Although we know that he is dreaming. We begin to hear a distant electrical hum, that continues and grows louder from this spot.

SUPERIMPOSE:

185 EXT. UNION SQUARE - DAY 185

PANNING VIEW ON ANN

Speaking thought we cannot hear. She seems terrified. The hum grows louder.

DISSOLVE:

186 CLOSE ON HARRY 186

He opens his eyes; he is sweating and his lips are dry. He looks, anxious, at the spot where Meredith was sleeping. She is gone. The hum continues.

187 FULL VIEW 187

Harry looks around the room, anxious over Meredith's disappearance. He gets up from the sofa, stumbling and cold; wrapping the blanket around him. The hum is ever-present. He moves through the warehouse; turns off the flapping recorder. Shuts off the amplifier.

He looks at the bench and can see the evidence that Meredith has been through some of his things. Some of the drawers are opened, and some papers are out.

HARRY
(calling out)
Meredith?

No answer. The hum continues.
Harry moves closer to the telephone, and the hum grows louder. The receiver is ajar. He pushes it with his forefinger, and the receiver falls onto the cradle with a dull sound, discontinuing the hum.

(CONTINUED)

187 CONTINUED: 187

HARRY
(realizing that he's been had)
Bitch!

FADE OUT:

FADE IN:
188 EXT. GOLDEN GATE PARK - DAY 188

VIEW ON THE BANDSHELL

The Municipal band in white uniforms plays a march behind an easel with a large number "7".

189 VIEW ON HARRY 189

Making his way through the park, apparently looking for someone. He carries his blue plastic pouch. Crosses onto the audience area.

190 VIEW ON THE CROWD 190

Sitting on benches under the shadows of the trees, while occasional men in jackets hand out long strip programs of the day. Harry moves up and down the shady corridors looking for someone. He refuses a program.

191 HARRY'S VIEW 191

Most of the people sitting here are very, very old.

192 CLOSE ON HARRY 192

Looking across to the other side.

193 HARRY'S VIEW 193

Stanley, dressed in jacket and tie, sitting next to an extremely old woman...talking to her occasionally.

194 MEDIUM VIEW 194

Harry moves across, toward them.

STANLEY
(seeing Harry)
Harry! What are you doing here?

HARRY
I want to talk to you.

(CONTINUED)

194 CONTINUED: 194

STANLEY
You remember my mother?

HARRY
(nods to the old woman, who remains rapt in the concert music throughout the scene.)

Nice to see you. Nice concert.

Harry sits next to Stanley on the bench.

HARRY
That girl who works for Moran went through my things.

STANLEY
What girl are you talking about Harry? Moran doesn't have any girls working for him.

HARRY
You know the one, Stanley...She left in the middle of the night. Fooled around with my phone; went through my files and my cabinets.

STANLEY
JeSUS, Harry.

HARRY
And what about you, Stanley? Why'd he hire you? For your brains?

STANLEY
Harry, cut it out; for Chrissakes!

HARRY
(rising, angrily)
But I didn't have any of my important stuff where she looked. It's all hidden away; and I'm changing all the locks, Stanley, so you can shove your keys up your ass!

STANLEY
Harry, my mother...

HARRY
Just stay away from me, and stay away from the warehouse. And tell that to Moran.

(CONTINUED)

194 CONTINUED: 194

Harry backs away a few steps, livid. Stanley's mother who has been oblivious to the argument the whole time, turns and smiles and then turns back to the concert.

STANLEY
Harry, what do you take...

HARRY
Just stay away from me...

CUT TO:

195 EXT. THE FINANCIAL DISTRICT - DAY 195

Sunday. The district is quiet, white and deserted. Large new buildings empty. The plazas and courtyards without people. We SEE a single man cross the street on his way to the Financial building.

196 HIGH ANGLE 196

The intersection, normally crowded with people and cars, now totally bare, accented by the white road markings and bus stops. Harry Caul crosses the intersection and makes his way to the patterned sidewalk which designates the Financial building.

CUT TO:

197 INT. PLAZA AREA - DAY 197

HIGH ANGLE

Harry continues under a large archway and crosses into the plaza. We HEAR footsteps echoing around the area.

CUT TO:

198 INT. ELEVATOR - DAY 198

HIGH ANGLE

Harry crosses into the empty elevator area. He stops by a security guard, signs a clipboard, and continues to the elevator.

CUT TO:

199 INT. THE ELEVATOR - DAY 199

Empty save Harry. He holds the blue vinyl pouch that we know holds the tape.

CUT TO:

200 INT. THE LOBBY - DAY 200

The bell clinks. Harry steps out into the main lobby. No one sits at the reception desk. He proceeds to the desk and up the spiral staircase.

CUT TO:

201 INT. THE LOBBY - DAY 201

Harry enters; the once busy maze is now totally empty. We can hear a distorted Latin-American song being played.

202 PANNING VIEW ON HARRY 202

He passes a janitor, busy at work, who keeps a transistor radio on his wagon. The janitor pays no attention to Harry. He continues along, turns to a new corridor. We HEAR a strange thumping sound moving toward us. Harry hears it, hesitates, and then moves on.

Then from around the corner, a large, black Doberman Pincher--obviously a trained attack dog--appears at the corridor. It quietly regards Harry.

203 VIEW ON HARRY 203

Stops. Doesn't say anything, but doesn't seem outwardly frightened.

204 VIEW ON THE DOG 204

Standing quietly at the end of the corridor, watching him.

205 MEDIUM VIEW 205

Harry moves ahead slowly, ingnoring the animal. He stops by a closed door. The dog moves closer, possessively, but does not growl.

Harry knocks quietly. There's no answer.

Once again; still no answer.

Harry turns to the dog, who stands by quietly, watching every move. Slowly, Harry opens the door revealing a large desk that commands a very large office. No one sits behind it.

CUT TO:

206 INT. THE DIRECTOR'S OFFICE - DAY 206

We can HEAR the sound of running water. Harry looks to his left and sees a man in his early fifties, Mr. C., rinsing out some cups and saucers in a small office, kitchenette.

HARRY
Hello.

The man doesn't react. Harry steps a little closer, speaks louder.

HARRY
HELLO.

Mr. C. turns, acknowledges Harry. He is not necessarily very old, but he carries something with him that is old, wise and perhaps laden with years of great power.

MR. C.
I didn't hear you.

He finishes rinsing off some cups, and then he closes the panelled doors which conceal the kitchenette. He seems as though he is in a state of physical pain every time he moves.

MR. C.
I didn't hear you.

He moves to the desk, opens a drawer, and puts a hearing aid on. Then he sits down.

The dog moves to the middle of the floor, and rests. Mr. C. pushes a button by the desk and nods to Harry.

MR. C.
Sit down.

Harry does, near the desk; the blue pouch in his lap.

MR. C.
You were able to do it?

HARRY
(taking the tape out of the pouch)
It went very well.

MR. C.
Speak louder.

(CONTINUED)

206 CONTINUED: 206

HARRY
(speaking loud)
I said it went very well.

MR. C.
(referring to his hearing aid)
These things don't work.

HARRY
(speaking loud)
Let me see.

Mr. C. hands the instrument to Harry, who puts it on his lap and gives it a look. Finally, he blows through the tubing and listens several times.

HARRY
(speaking loud)
You have to keep the transducer tubes clean. Blow it out every once in a while.

In the middle of this discussion, the door quietly opens and the young man, Martin, enters, locks the door and places a small tape recorder down on the desk. He proceeds to plug it in and make it ready to play.

MR. C.
Thanks.

He reaches into his drawer and pulls out an envelope filled with Harry's payment.

MR. C.
I'm sorry about Friday; I had to go to Madrid.

HARRY
You instructed me not to turn it over to anyone but you.

MR. C.
You were right.

He gives what could be interpreted as a severe look to Martin, who does not flinch.

Mr. C. waits as Harry methodically counts the bills, then looks up and nods.

(CONTINUED)

206 CONTINUED: 206

MR. C.
Play it.

Harry looks up toward Martin.

MR. C.
Go ahead, play it. I want him
to hear it.

Harry threads the tape on the recorder. Looks to both of these men, and then turns it on.

207 CLOSE VIEW ON MR. C. 207

Watching carefully.

ANN (o.s.)
"...Wake up, wake up you sleepy head,
Get up, get up, get out of bed..."

208 CLOSE VIEW ON MARTIN 208

ANN (o.s.)
"...Cheer up, cheer up, the sun is red,
Live, love, laugh and be happy..."

209 VIEW ON HARRY 209

ANN (o.s.)
You got a quarter?
I don't know what to get him
for Christmas, he's already got
everything.

MARK (o.s.)
He doesn't need anything...anymore.

Harry notices something on an office cabinet near Mr. Mr. C.

ANN (o.s.)
I haven't decided ...(static) what
to get you yet.

210 HARRY'S VIEW 210

A nicely framed photograph of Ann.

MARK (o.s.)
Better start looking.

CUT TO:

211 CLOSE VIEW 211

The photograph of Ann.

The view PANS to another photograph showing Mr. C. and Ann, arm in arm, having just gotten off a plane.

212 MEDIUM VIEW 212

Mr. C. notices Harry looking at the photograph.

MR. C.
Her name is Ann.

He glances up at Martin.

ANN (o.s.)
Well...
(pause)
Well, what about me?

MARK (o.s.)
You'll see.

MR. C.
(to Harry)
It's very clear.

HARRY
Thank you.

Harry feels awkward in the room as the three of them listen to the tape. There is some unspoken tension between Mr. C. and Martin; as though hearing his tape is to settle some disagreement between them.

ANN (o.s.)
You're no fun. You're supposed to tease me, give me hints. You know.

MARK (o.s.)
Does it bother you?

ANN (o.s.)
What?

MARK (o.s.)
Walking around in circles.

ANN (o.s.)
Look, that's terrible.

(CONTINUED)

213 VIEW ON MR. C. 213

Listening; every once in while looking up at his Assistant.

MARK (o.s.)
He's not hurting anyone.

ANN (o.s.)
Neither are we...Oh, God.

214 VIEW ON MARTIN 214

As though he's been waiting for something incriminating to be said.

ANN (o.s.)
Every time I see one of them, I always think the same thing...

MARK (o.s.)
What do you think?

215 VIEW ON MR. C. 215

ANN (o.s.)
I think he was somebody's baby boy, and they loved him.

He turns to look at her picture.

216 VIEW ON THE PORTRAIT 216

ANN (o.s.)
...and here he is now, half-dead on a park bench and where is his mother or his father or his uncles.

217 VIEW ON HARRY 217

Waiting. His duty to remain and answer any questions.

ANN (o.s.)
...anyway, that's what I always think.

MARK
...I guess I think of how when they had a newspaper strike in New York, more of those old drunks died
cont'd.

MR. C.
(to Martin)
This is what they talk about.

(CONTINUED)

217 CONTINUED: 217

MARK (o.s.)
in one night because they didn't have newspapers to cover themselves with. Fifty of them froze to death in one night.

MARTIN
I'm sure there's more.
(to Harry)
Am I right?

ANN (o.s.)
Just because there were no newspapers?

MR. C.
(suddenly very angry)
You WANT it to be true!

MARK (o.s.)
Really, it keeps them warm.

MARTIN
(defensively)
Of course not. I just want you to know... everything you should know.

ANN (o.s.)
That's terrible.

MARK (o.s.)
Who started this conversation, anyhow?

ANN (o.s.)
You did.

MARK (o.s.)
I did not.

Harry notices that when Mr. C's anger flashes, Martin backs down quietly.

ANN (o.s.)
You did too. You just don't remember.
(pause)
Mark...it's all right...we can talk.

MARK (o.s.)
I can't stand it.

218 VIEW ON MR. C. 218

Listening.

ANN (o.s.)
You're going to make my cry.

MARK (o.s.)
I know, honey. I know.
(pause)
Me too...

(CONTINUED)

218 CONTINUED: 218

Mr. C. listens to this intimacy.

ANN (o.s.)
No...don't.

MARK (o.s.)
Oh, God....

219 VIEW ON MARTIN 219

MARTIN
(politely)
Should I repeat that part?

MR. C.
No.

ANN (o.s.)
Take a bite out of your sandwich
and pretend I just told you a joke.
(they laugh)

Mr. C. suddenly turns in his swivel chair; his back facing Harry and Martin.

MARK (o.s.)
Where'd you hear that?

ANN (o.s.)
My secret.

MARK (o.s.)
How do you feel?

HARRY
(tentatively, he
knows he shouldn't)
It could mean ...it
could mean anything.
(he look up to Martin
who seems satisfied
and doesn't answer)
Is she...is she your
wife?

MARK (o.s.)
It's a nice day today; yesterday
it was cold and foggy.

22Ø VIEW ON HARRY 22Ø

Unable to stop himself from asking these questions.

HARRY
Well...well what will you do?

ANN (o.s.)
Do you think we can do it?

MARK (o.s.)
Later in the week. Sunday, maybe.

(CONTINUED)

220 CONTINUED: 220

HARRY
Today is Sunday.

221 VIEW ON MR. C. 221

Turns around in his chair. It seems as though he has been crying.

ANN (o.s.)
Sunday definitely...

MARK (o.s.)
...3 o'clock, Room B-7, Continental Lodge.

HARRY
(frightened)
What will you do to them? I'm responsible for this.

CUT TO:

222 EXT. THE PARK - DAY 222

She has just noticed Paul following them. The familiar look of fear comes to her face.

ANN
Look. See him? The one with the hearing aid...like...

MARK
No. Where?

ANN
He was following us. He kept following us close.

MARK
It's nothing; don't worry about it.

CUT TO:

223 INT. THE OFFICE - DAY 223

CLOSE VIEW ON THE DOG

It gets to its feet.

ANN (o.s.)
"When the red, red robin,
Goes bob, bob, bobbin' along..."

CUT TO:

224 MOVING VIEW 224

Harry is being shown out of the office by Martin. We SEE Mr. C. alone at the desk, receding into the background, as does the sound from the tape.

ANN (o.s.)
God, it will be so good to be finished with this.

I love you...

Martin closes the door on the image of Mr. C.

CUT TO:

225 INT. THE ELEVATOR - DAY 225

Martin puts his arm into the closing elevator for a moment. Harry looks out at him from the elevator.

MARTIN
Fifteen thousand. That's really nice for an afternoon's work.
(pause)
Forget it, Mr. Caul. Forget it.

HARRY
What will he do to them?

Martin finally pulls his hand from the bobbing door, letting it close on Harry and on his question.

CUT TO:

226 EXT. THE FINANCIAL DISTRICT - DAY 226

Bleak and desolate.
Harry walks along the plaza, alone.

227 MOVING VIEW ON HARRY 227

As he walks, he seems to be in an emotional quandary, raging over the role he has played in this. He walks blindly in a straight line.

228 MEDIUM VIEW 228

The empty commercial plaza. Harry alone, walking. He stops by an all-glass telephone booth. Quickly, he steps in it and closes the door, sitting on a small, built-in bench. He is breathing hard. He calms himself and pulls himself together in the privacy of the glass booth.

CUT TO:

229 FULL VIEW 229

Harry huddled in the telephone booth.

CUT TO:

230 INT. A CATHOLIC CHURCH 230

There are a few people in the church, but the last Mass is long over.

Harry dips his hand in the basin of Holy Water, crosses himself, and moves to the area near the Confessional. He waits quietly, the blue pouch on his lap. Nearby, above him, is a large statue of Mary.

A ten year old boy leaves the Confessional and runs too quickly out of the Church. Harry steps in.

CUT TO:

231 INT. THE CONFESSIONAL - DAY 231

Harry kneels in the dark confessional. We barely see the ear of the Priest through the wooden grating.

HARRY
(quietly)
Bless me, Father, for I have sinned. It is three months since my last confession.
(pause)
I...my sins are these:
(pause)
I have...used the name of our Lord in vain on several occasions. I... umm...on a number of occasions, I took newspapers from their racks without paying for them. I have... I have deliberately taken pleasure in...impure thoughts. I...I have committed a willful impure act... on myself...on several occasions.
(he pauses, breathes, nad then, very quickly)
For these and all the sins of my past life I am heartily sorry...

CUT TO:

232 EXT. CONTINENTAL LODGE - DAY 232

The neon sign of the Motel lit up against the daylight. A smaller sign blinks "Vacancy" on and off.

CUT TO:

233 THE VIEW ALTERS 233

We watch Harry standing across the street from the Motel.

234 CLOSE VIEW ON HARRY 234

Standing alone opposite the motel, just waiting and looking.

235 HARRY'S VIEW 235

(interrupted by traffic)
The Motel. He scans the various windows of the second floor, their windows curtained closed.

236 FULL VIEW 236

Harry crosses the street, and enters the Motel office.

CUT TO:

237 INT. THE MOTEL LOBBY - DAY 237

Harry has entered the lobby, is speaking to the clerk.

CLERK
B-7's spoken for.

Harry doesn't answer.

CLERK
They're all the same.

Still he's silent.

CLERK
Well?

HARRY
Give me the one next to it.

CUT TO:

238 INT. MOTEL CORRIDOR - DAY 238

CLOSE MOVING ANGLE

On Harry as he walks down the corridor. He approaches the door B-7. There is a DO NOT DISTURB SIGN hanging on the doorknob. Harry continues on past, moves on to room B-5. He uses the motel key and opens the door and enters.

CUT TO:

239 INT. MOTEL ROOM - DAY 239

Harry walks into the sterile motel room, stright to the rear window, which has a two-foot terrace. He steps out, peeks to the side.

240 HARRY'S VIEW 240

The windows of B-7 are closed.

241 VIEW ON THE ROOM 241

Harry moves across the room, and into the bathroom. He presses his hear against the wall.

242 CLOSE ON HARRY 242

Listening.

The faintest suggestion of voices coming from the room. Harry sits on the bathroom floor, and opens his small attache case. He takes out a jeweler's drill, and slowly and very quietly drills through to the next room.

Then he takes a tiny, pellet-like instrument, connected by spider thin wires, and pokes it into the small hole. He takes a small earphone, and quickly attaches the wires to a small electrical box, and then, in an uncomfortable position under the sink, listens.

243 FULL VIEW 243

There is something ridiculous in this view of Harry, huddled under the sink.

THE VIEW MOVES CLOSER TO HIM, as it gets nearer we HEAR what he hears, progressively louder.

ANN (o.s.)
Everytime I see one of them, I always think the same thing.

MARK (o.s.)
What do you think?

ANN (o.s.)
I think he's someone's baby. Don't laugh, really I do.

Harry's eyes widen with horror, as slowly he, as we, realize that we are listening to the same conversation.

(CONTINUED)

243 CONTINUED: 243

ANN (o.s.)
I think he was someone's baby boy and they loved him and here he is now, half-dead on a park bench...

WE ARE EXTREMELY CLOSE ON HARRY, and the conversation is very LOUD.

Harry pulls the earphone from his ear and steps away from the sink. By now, he isn't sure if this is a distortion in his mind, or in fact happening in the next room.

Now there is a dull LOUD noise muffled from B-7, then a barely audible shout.

244 VIEW ON HARRY 244

He steps away, into the motel room.

245 CLOSE ON HARRY 245

A girl's voice is speaking at a high pitch, and then a terrible human groan. It is all so faint, Harry isn't sure if it's real or not. He backs further away from these sounds. Something crashing to the floor, and now a repeated dull blow of violence over and over again.

Harry throws his hands over his ears, trying to shut it out, but it persists.

246 VIEW ON HARRY'S WALL 246

A typical motel wall with commercial decor. From the other side outrageous sounds of violence.

247 VIEW ON HARRY 247

He turns to the motel television and turns in on LOUD. But somehow, the sounds of terror from the next room seem to persist.

248 FULL VIEW 248

Harry backs to one of the twin beds of his motel room, and fully dressed, crawls under the blanket, squeezing the pillow around his hears.

CUT TO:

249 CLOSE VIEW ON HARRY 249

The pillow clasped over his ears; MUSIC from the television playing LOUD in the room. His eyes, furtive and nervous, not knowing if the atrocity he imagines in the next room has concluded or not.

Then he turns his face over, into the bed.

250 FULL VIEW 250

Harry buries himself in the fed. The television continues to play its MUSIC.

DISSOLVE:

251 INT. HARRY'S MOTEL ROOM - NIGHT 251

The television, still tuned LOUDLY, now plays a talk show. Harry turns, having passed out or fallen asleep. He discovers himself in the bed, in his clothes. He looks up.

252 VIEW ON THE TELEVISION 252

Men around a panel: volume up loud.

253 MEDIUM VIEW 253

Harry steps out of bed, shuts off the television. Quickly, he remembers the circumstances, pulls his things together and moves to the door.

CUT TO:

254 INT. THE CORRIDOR - NIGHT 254

Harry moves from his room, to the door B-7. The DO NOT DISTURB sign is gone.

Harry knocks quietly on the door. There is no answer. He reaches into his pocket, takes out a ring of picks, and easily opens the lock.

CUT TO:

255 INT. B-7 MOTEL ROOM - NIGHT 255

The door opens into the room and cautiously, Harry steps in.

256 CLOSE ON HARRY 256

Closing the door behind him, he looks at the room.

CUT TO:

257 HARRY'S VIEW 257

Perfectly made up, as though no one had been there at all.

258 CLOSE ON HARRY 258

Surprised, confused.

259 HARRY'S VIEW 259

The beds, perfectly neat, up on the wall, the little tray with coffee cups wrapped in tissue paper. Not a trace, not a sign of anyone having been there. We begin to HEAR a high sound, we do not recognize as yet.

260 MEDIUM VIEW 260

Harry steps into the room; the various little card-board notices are placed around advertising this or that, ready for the next guests. Harry moves more quickly, looking for some hint, some confirmation of what he heard. But there is nothing. He moves to the bathroom, enters.

CUT TO:

261 INT. THE BATHROOM - DAY 261

The sound we heard is louder here. But still not recognizable. Harry looks around the room; it is totally clean. The glasses are wrapped in paper, the soap is new, wrapped in its advertisement. The toilet has the paper band around it marked, "Sanitized for your protection."

Harry looks up.

262 HARRY'S VIEW 262

The shower curtain is pulled closed.

263 MEDIUM VIEW 263

Harry lifts his arm, about to pull back the curtain. He hesitates momentarily, afraid of what he might find there. He pulls it.

264 VIEW ON THE BATHTUB 264

Empty. Perfectly clean. Harry leans over, and runs his finger by the drain. Brings up to see, but there is no tell-tale drop of blood.

(CONTINUED)

264 CONTINUED: 264

Harry begins to doubt himself, what he heard. He begins to leave the bathroom when that annoying, ever-present sound stops him. He turns, realizes that it is the water re-fill on the toilet. He bends over, and lifts the seat, breaking its paper seal. Like everything else, it was immaculately cleaned.

He jiggles the flush handle to free it and the toilet flushes.

265 CLOSE ON HARRY 265

Looking. Then, suddenly the familiar look of horror sweeps over him. He is terrified.

266 VIEW OVER HARRY TO THE TOILET 266

It had been clogged; suddenly, the water in the bowl turns blood-red and begins to rise.

267 VIEW ON HARRY 267

Frozen to this spot; understanding that what he HEARD, actually took place.

268 HIGH ANGLE 268

The bloodied water keeps coming, spilling out onto the tile floor, over to Harry's shoes. He instinctively lifts one foot, stepping away from it as though it were contaminated, leaving vivid blood-red footsteps wherever he moves.

269 INT. B-7 MOTEL ROOM - DAY 269

He moves, blindly, out into the main room, seeing his own trail of bloody footsteps. He staggers by the window, pulls up the half-closed blinds, and opens the window for cool air.

CUT TO:

27Ø EXT. THE MOTEL - DAY 27Ø

VIEW ON HARRY

Breathing deeply. He would scream out, but he is unable.

CUT TO:

271 EXT. THE FINANCIAL PLAZA - DAY 271

FULL VIEW

The plaza is alive with people. Harry moves quickly through the crowds.

He stops and looks up.

272 HARRY'S VIEW 272

The tall, white monolith.

CUT TO:

273 INT. THE DIRECTOR'S RECEPTION AREA - DAY 273

The elevator light clinks on, doors open, and Harry proceeds directly past the reception desk, toward the Director's office.

RECEPTIONIST
Excuse me.

Harry doesn't stop. The receptionist hurries after him.

RECEPTIONIST
EXCUSE ME.

274 MOVING VIEW ON HARRY 274

Continuing on. The receptionist continues along with him.

RECEPTIONIST
I'll have to announce you.

HARRY
I'm going to see the Director.

RECEPTIONIST
He isn't here; we don't expect him today. What's your name?

HARRY
Harry Caul.

RECEPTIONIST
I'll have him contact you.

HARRY
(pushing him and moving on)
I have to see him NOW.

(CONTINUED)

274 CONTINUED: 274

RECEPTIONIST

Guard!

Harry moves on to the Director's door. He opens it.

275 HARRY'S VIEW 275

The office is empty.

RECEPTIONIST

Will you leave?

The Guard stands in place, his hand on the pistol. Harry looks at both of them, and then moves directly toward the lobby.

CUT TO:

276 INT. THE ELEVATOR - DAY 276

Harry is in the elevator going down. It stops, some people step in. It continues down. Stops again, more people, and then on down. The claustrophobia begins to move in on Harry, when suddenly he is shocked.

The elevator has stopped and Ann (the girl of the recorded conversation) steps in. The door closes and the elevator continues down.

277 VIEW ON ANN 277

Resting in the crowd. She does not recognize him, does not know him.

278 FULL VIEW 278

The elevator stops once again, and some people leave. It continues down.

279 VIEW ON HARRY 279

The elevator stops and more people get out.

Now they spend the substantial part of the descent alone. He looks away from her, then finally, closes his eyes.

280 VIEW ON ANN 280

She smiles at him cordially.

CUT TO:

281 VIEW ON HARRY 281

Ill-at-ease, he smiles back at her.

Finally, after what seemed an interminable time, the elevator arrives at the ground floor. He allows her to leave first, holding the door open for her.

ANN

Thank you.

CUT TO:

282 EXT. THE BUILDING - DAY 282

Ann walks out of the huge, corporate building, and down the street. Harry follow, hesistantly. He stands in front of the building, watching her.

283 HARRY'S VIEW 283

Ann moves toward the electric bus.

Low fog is blowing in through the city.
Harry stands petrified, as Ann walks quickly to an electric city bus, steps in. The bus silently pulls away. Fortunately, a second bus is right behind it. Harry hurries across the street and boards the second bus.

284 MOVING VIEW ON THE FIRST BUS 284

A ghostly image, moving silently through the low fog.

285 MOVING VIEW ON ANN 285

Sitting alone in the near empty bus.

286 MOVING VIEW ON THE ELECTRIC WIRES OVERHEAD 286

The feelers gliding along with a brittle sound, occasionally jumping, and creating a shower of sparks.

287 MOVING VIEW ON HARRY 287

In the second bus, sitting up at the head, looking forward through the window.

288 HARRY'S POINT OF VIEW 288

The rear of the first bus. Moving through the fog silently.

CUT TO:

289 MOVING VIEW OF THE FIRST BUS 289

Climbing a steep hill. We can still see Ann.

290 MOVING VIEW ON THE OVERHEAD WIRES 290

Coming apart, then joining.

291 MOVING VIEW ON THE FIRST BUS 291

Making a turn to the right.

292 MOVING VIEW ON THE SECOND BUS 292

Climbing the hill, silently.

293 MOVING VIEW ON HARRY 293

Watching the bus with Ann on it.

294 MOVING VIEW ON THE OVERHEAD WIRES 294

The antennae glide along the grid, going straight.

295 MOVING VIEW ON THE SECOND BUS 295

It fails to make the turn, continuing straight ahead.

296 VIEW ON HARRY 296

Standing.

HARRY
I have to get off.

DRIVER
Next block.

HARRY
I have to get off!

Harry presses against the electric doors; they spring open.

CUT TO:

297 EXT. VIEW ON THE BUS - LATE DAY 297

Harry stumbles out of the electric doors while the bus is still moving. He hits the ground still clutching his case. The Driver stops the bus when he realizes what has happened, but Harry is quickly up and running toward the first bus, which has momentarily stopped to let off some passengers.

CUT TO:

298 INT. THE BUS - LATE DAY 298

Harry breathlessly climbs onto the bus, sweating, and dirty from his fall.

The bus silently continues forward as Harry makes his way down the aisle, trying to keep his balance.

He sits one seat behind Ann, who has not paid more than cursory attention to Harry.

CUT TO:

299 EXT. THE BUS - LATE DAY 299

MOVING VIEW

Slowly and quietly the bus moves through the thickening fog.

CUT TO:

300 INT. THE BUS - LATE DAY 300

MEDIUM VIEW

Harry leans forward, behind Ann.

HARRY
Ann.

She is startled by the sound of her name. Instinctively frightened, she turns back and sees Harry: unfamiliar, sweaty and imploring. She turns away.

HARRY
Please... listen to me.

ANN
(frightened)
Who are you?

HARRY
We've never met, but I know you;
I know who you are and I know about
your problem.

301 CLOSE VIEW ON ANN 301

She listens, then quickly rises, moving forward in the moving bus.

CUT TO:

302 NEW VIEW 302

She takes another seat on the opposite side of the bus. Harry sighs, and moves to the seat behind her. All the following is whispered.

HARRY
Don't be afraid of me.

ANN
How do you know my name?

HARRY
I've listened to you...to the two of you.

She looks back at him; her look is severe and accusing.

ANN
What problem...I have no problem.

CUT TO:

303 EXT. THE BUS - NIGHT 303

MOVING VIEW

A ghostly silent image.

304 MOVING VIEW THROUGH THE WINDOW 304

Harry sitting behind Ann. He is silent for a moment. She turns, looking forward, ignoring him.

CUT TO:

305 INT. THE BUS - NIGHT 305

VIEW ON ANN

Looking forward, Harry leans toward her whispering.

HARRY
You have to understand...that I... myself have nothing to do with this...

ANN
(without looking back)
Please go away...

HARRY
I am not responsible, in any way. But, I can't stand by...

(CONTINUED)

305 CONTINUED: 305

ANN
What are you talking about?

HARRY
I was worried about you...I thought
that something terrible...

ANN
You're frightening me...

HARRY
...something terrible. Because I
feel something for you, even...

ANN
Go away; please go away.

HARRY
...though I don't know you, you're
so familiar. Someone I've known
so intimately...

ANN
Driver...

HARRY
...and care for; I feel as though
I've known you for a long time.

Ann moves to the front of the bus.

ANN
(to the Driver)
This man...please, he's bothering me.

Harry follows her, as though trying to prove his loyalty.

HARRY
Everytime I see one of them, I
always think the same thing...

DRIVER
What IS this? Come on!

HARRY
I think...he was somebody's baby...
I think he was somebody's baby boy,
and they loved him.

CUT TO:

306 VIEW ON ANN 306

Shocked as she recognizes what Harry is saying.

DRIVER
Quit it, will you.

HARRY
...and here he is now, half-dead on a park bench.

DRIVER
Alright. Off the bus. Off the bus.

He pulls the bus over; and Ann quickly uses this opportunity to run out of the bus.

HARRY
Wait...please...

CUT TO:

307 EXT. THE STREET - NIGHT 307

Ann runs awkwardly down a steep street, away from the bus. Her shoes are difficult to maneuver on the many shallow concrete steps cut into the steep grade. Harry takes a few steps, looking down at her.

HARRY
(shouting)
I want to HELP you!

He looks back.

308 HARRY'S VIEW 308

The driver has stepped out of the bus, which stands in the middle of the street.

DRIVER
Hey! Do you want me to call the Police? You hear me!

309 MOVING VIEW ON HARRY 309

He begins, hesitantly, to run down the many steps, two at a time, to catch up with Ann. He is breathless and middle-aged.

CUT TO:

310 NEW VIEW 310

Ann's high-heel shoes click awkwardly down the steps. She is still a good distance away from him. She turns back, as she moves.

ANN
Please leave me alone.

311 VIEW UP THE STEPPED STREET 311

Harry on the street. A distance behind him, the electric bus waits like some immobile monster; the driver standing in a momentary indecisiveness. Harry raises his arms, unable to articulate his strong emotion; then finally:

HARRY
I'm a good man.

312 HARRY'S VIEW 312

She turns and continues down the steps.

313 VIEW ON HARRY 313

HARRY
I'm a good man.

Harry moves down the steps.

314 HIS VIEW 314

She has made it to the base of the street, turns, and is out of sight.

315 CLOSE ON HARRY 315

Terrified that he might lose her.

316 LOW FULL ANGLE 316

Harry alone, moving quickly down the steps.

CUT TO:

317 EXT. THE PARK - NIGHT 317

MEDIUM VIEW

We look up to the symmetrical green terracing; clean and simple. Two rows of grey steps cut up to the top. We SEE the small figure of Ann, moving up the second

(CONTINUED)

317 CONTINUED: 317

row and into the park. Harry watches, then he begins to move up the steps.

318 CLOSE ON HARRY 318

Moving up the steps. He watches her.

319 HARRY'S VIEW 319

Ann stands high on the second level of the park. She is frightened, but she stands motionless, watching him.

320 MEDIUM VIEW 320

Harry has arrived on the first level, she starts to walk along the top. He walks along with her, one level below; afraid that she will run away if he moves any closer.

321 MOVING VIEW ACROSS HARRY TO ANN 321

HARRY
My name is Harry Caul. I live here in the city, in an apartment building that I own. 220 Polk Street.
(suddenly)
Can you hear me? Are you listening?

There is no reaction from her. She keeps walking slowly.

HARRY
I would tell you more about myself... but there's so little. I...never did well. When I was younger, I never did well at school. My father wanted me to be a printer, so he'd be sure I could make a living. He went to college, and was disappointed in me.

322 VIEW ON ANN 322

She doesn't look at him. Fog is blowing across the levels of the park.

HARRY (o.s.)
My mother was Roman Catholic...

CUT TO:

323 VIEW ON HARRY 323

Almost passionately telling her these things.

HARRY
I was very sick when I was a boy.
I was paralyzed in my left arm and
my left leg, and couldn't walk for
six months.
I remember...when one doctor told
me that I'd never be able to walk
again.

324 VIEW ACROSS TO ANN 324

The fog momentarily causes her to disappear, then come back.

HARRY
...My mother used to lower me
into a hot bath...it was therapy.
Once the doorbell rang, and she
left me propped on the tub, while
she answered it. I could hear her
talking downstairs while I began to
slip into the water.

325 VIEW ON HARRY 325

HARRY
...I felt the water up to my chin,
and my mouth, and my nose...and then
my eyes. I remember I could see under
the water. But I couldn't lift myself
out of it. I remember I wasn't afraid.
When I woke up later, my skin was
greasy from the holy oil she had rubbed
on my body...
And I remember being disappointed that
I had survived.

326 VIEW ON ANN 326

Faintly there.

HARRY (o.s.)
I like to eat...but I've never
liked potatoes.

327 VIEW ON HARRY 327

Moving.

(CONTINUED)

327 CONTINUED: 327

HARRY
...When I was five years old, I was introduced to a friend of my father's and for no reason at all, I hit him with all my strength in his stomach. He died a year later.

Harry sits on a small bench in the path.

...He had an ulcer...But my father always said that he died partly because of me. My mother said he would have died anyway.

When I was four, I took a puppy I loved and hit it over the head with a toy hammer.

I hated a Nun because she slapped me...but I loved the Virgin Mary because she gave me anything I wanted whenever I prayed to her.

318 VIEW ON ANN 318

Standing, disappearing, returning.

HARRY (o.s.)
On my thirty-sixth birthday, as a birthday present to myself...

329 VIEW ON HARRY 329

On the bench, no longer looking at her.

HARRY
...I turned in a false alarm. And I remember a girl named Marjorie who kissed me on the lips and told me she loved me on the day her family was moving back to Virginia because her father was an officer in the Navy.

330 VIEW ON ANN 330

Standing, disappearing...now gone.

HARRY (o.s.)
...I am miserly and cheap, and penny pinching...

CUT TO:

331 VIEW ON HARRY 331

HARRY
...I enjoy looking at my face in the mirror. I am not afraid of death...but I am afraid of murder.

Silence. Harry looks up to the second terrace. It is covered with fog.

Are you there?

332 FULL VIEW 332

Harry alone, sitting on the bench.

FADE OUT:

FADE IN:
333 EXT. HARRY'S WAREHOUSE ALLEY - NIGHT 333

CLOSE MOVING SHOT

Harry as he walks slowly down the quiet alleyway of his warehouse. He stops, having noticed something.

334 MEDIUM VIEW 334

Harry looking up at his warehouse; the rows of flourescent lights are burning.

335 HARRY'S VIEW 335

The wire-reinforced windows. Lighted.

336 VIEW ON HARRY 336

He moves toward the elevator door; then thinks against that. Unlocks and enters the steel stair-case.

CUT TO:

337 INT. HARRY'S WAREHOUSE - NIGHT 337

Harry at the base of the staircase. He looks up.

338 HARRY'S VIEW 338

Someone is in the warehouse; occasionally there is a voice, and the noise of movement.

CUT TO:

339 MEDIUM VIEW 339

Cautiously, frightened, Harry begins to move up the steel staircase, extra careful not to make a sound.

340 NEW VIEW 340

At the warehouse level. Harry slowly approaching.

341 VIEW ON HARRY 341

Without realizing it, Harry's foot dislodges a beercan that was on one of the steps.

342 CLOSE ON HARRY 342

Realizing what he's done.

343 HIS VIEW 343

The can goes tumbling down the steel steps, echoing as it falls.

342 VIEW ON HARRY 344

Looking up toward the warehouse. The lights go out. Harry gasps, then takes several more steps and hesitates. Silence, then in a whisper.

HARRY
Who is it?

No answer. Harry steps up the last few steps, and onto the main floor of the warehouse.

HARRY
What do you want?

We HEAR movement, but there is no answer.

HARRY
(terrified)
What are you doing here?

A moment of silence and then, out of the darkness, laughter.

MARK (o.s.)
Who told you that one, Mr. C.?

ANN (o.s.)
Who else?

CUT TO:

345 CLOSE ON HARRY 345

Frightened.

HARRY
Who's there?

MARK (o.s.)
How do you feel?

ANN (o.s.)
Oh, you know.

MARK (o.s.)
It's a nice day today; yesterday it was cold and foggy.

HARRY
Who...

There is sound of movement. Harry is startled. It is the sound of the elevator going down.

ANN (o.s.)
Can we do it?

MARK (o.s.)
Later in the week. Friday maybe.

Harry runs to the side wall; switches on the light.

346 CLOSE ON HARRY 346

Temporarily blinded, he shields his eyes.

347 WHAT HE SEES 347

The warehouse. All its secrets examined: its drawers and cabinets. The devices; opened and examined; blueprints, circuitry. And the master tape turning.

ANN (o.s.)
Sunday, definitely...

MARK (o.s.)
The Continental...3 o'clock. B-7.

Harry moves to the warehouse window. Looks out.

ANN (o.s.)
Look. See him? The one with the hearing aid...like...

(CONTINUED)

347 CONTINUED: 347

MARK (o.s.)
No...where?

348 HARRY'S VIEW 348

Two men have left the building and walk quickly down, and then around the corner.

ANN (o.s.)
He was following us. He kept following us close.

HARRY

(shouting down)
Moran! I know it's you.

The men don't look up. Harry shouts down again, pathetically.

Moran, is it you?

The men disappear.

MARK (o.s.)
It's nothing. Don't worry about it.

349 MEDIUM VIEW 348

Harry turns back toward the warehouse, and the recorder.

ANN (o.s.)
God, it will be so good to be finished with this.
(static and muffled sound)

Harry moves to the recorder.

ANN (o.s.)
I love you.

He switches it off. Turns it to rewind.

350 CLOSE ON THE RECORDER 350

Rewinding.

351 CLOSE ON HARRY 351

Waiting. Then something hits him.

(CONTINUED)

351 CONTINUED: 351

HARRY
What?

He stops the tape; moves it fast forward, and stops it.

352 VIEW ON THE TAPE 352

Turning.

MARK (o.s.)
It's a nice day today; yesterday it was cold and foggy.

ANN (o.s.)
Do you think we can do it?

353 CLOSE ANGLE ON HARRY 353

Suddenly, these words have a new meaning for him.

MARK (o.s.)
Later in the week. Friday maybe.

CUT TO

353 INT. MOTEL BATHROOM - DAY 353

Harry's shoes make bloody footsteps on the tile floor, and the out to the carpet of the motel room.

ANN (o.s.)
Do you think we can do it?

CUT TO:

355 INT. HARRY'S WAREHOUSE - NIGHT 355

CLOSE ON HARRY

Remembering.

MARK (o.s.)
Later in the week...

CUT TO:

356 INT. MOTEL BATHROOM - DAY 356

THE BATHROOM

Wads of tissue paper soaked in blood are thrown into the toilet bowl, and flushed.

Ann moves back into the main room where Mark is busy washing the blood from the wall.

Ann efficiently removes the blood stained linen from the floor.

MARK (o.s.)
...Sunday maybe.

Near to them is the brutally wounded body of Mr. C. lying on a plastic sheet on one of the beds.

ANN (o.s.)
Sunday definitely.

CUT TO:

357 INT. HARRY'S WAREHOUSE - NIGHT 357
VIEW ON THE TAPE

Turning.

MARK (o.s.)
Continental Lodge. 3 o'clock.
Room B-7.

358 VIEW ON HARRY 358

Stepping away from the recorder, staring at it.

ANN (o.s.)
Look. See him? The one with the
hearing aide...like...

CUT TO:

359 INT. MOTEL ROOM - DAY 359

FULL VIEW

Mr. C. shouts in pain as Mark plunges a short-bladed knife into him. We don't hear any of these sounds, but must remember them from the time Harry heard them from the next room.

(CONTINUED)

359 CONTINUED: 359

Ann uses a small knife as well, screaming at the top of her lungs as she also stabs him. Blood splashes onto the little cablecar motif on the wall.

MARK (o.s.)
No. Where?

Mr. C. is in pain, and pounds both his hands on the wall.

ANN (o.s.)
He was following us. He kept following us close.

360 CLOSE ON ANN 360

Screaming. The blood of her husband is on her hands and face.

MARK (o.s.)
It's nothing, don't worry about it.

361 VIEW ON MARK 361

Mr. C. holds on to him, as Mark delivers the last blows. Mr. C. begins to slide to the floor.

ANN (o.s.)
"When the red, red robin,
Goes bob, bob, bobbin' along, along."

CUT TO:

362 INT. WAREHOUSE - NIGHT 362

VIEW ON HARRY

ANN (o.s.)
God, it will be so good to be finished with this...

CUT TO:

363 INT. MOTEL ROOM - DAY 363

Mr. C., angry and nervous, operates a small portable tape recorder for Mark and Ann.

ANN (o.s.)
I love you.

(CONTINUED)

363 CONTINUED: 363

Mark moves around him and locks the door.

CUT TO:

364 INT. THE WAREHOUSE - NIGHT 364

Harry shuts off the recorder.

CUT TO:

365 EXT. A STREET - DAY 365

A mangled automobile.

We are CLOSE on the body of Mr. C., slumped bleeding over the wheel of the crashed Mercedes. The automobile bursts into flame.

CUT TØ:

366 INT. MR. C'S BUILDING - DAY 366

CLOSE VIEW ON HARRY

Looking down.

367 WHAT HE SEES: 367

A stack of newspapers. The front page features a picture of the burnt-out Mercedes. Several people move past Harry; several papers are sold.

We can read a headline: "Executive Killed in Auto Accident."

CUT TO:

368 INT. FINANCIAL BUILDING LOBBY - DAY 368

MEDIUM VIEW

Harry is in the lobby of the financial building. Many people move past him in the newsstand area. He holds a pouch in his arms.

Harry moves toward the elevators.

CUT TO:

369 INT. THE RECEPTION AREA - DAY 369

Harry steps into the Reception area from the elevator. This offices feels the full weight of the recent tragedy. It seems as though there are many people from the press; more Guards have been put on to keep them and the involved and interested concerned in some sort of order.

Harry moves into this crowd, still holding his pouch. Phones are ringing, and there is a sense of confusion and disorder. Now a few people begin to appear from the main corridor. Some of the Press photographers spring to action; a rumble moves through the crowd.

370 CLOSE ON HARRY 370

Looking.

371 HIS VIEW 371

A few Security Guards lead a group of Mr. C.'s young associates. Then the widow, Ann, dressed in mourning moving quickly, and with the guards discouraging the inevitable photographs. Near to her, though trying to seem like one of the group of other young men, is Mark.

372 CLOSE ON ANN 372

As she moves, glancing to the crowd, she notices Harry.

373 MOVING VIEW PASSING HARRY 373

Looking at her.

374 VIEW ON ANN 374

Frightened, she turns to Mark and nods toward Harry.

375 VIEW ON MARK 375

He takes note of Harry.

376 MEDIUM VIEW 376

The Guards make room for this party of people. They enter the elevator.

CUT TO:

377 INT. HARRY'S APARTMENT - NIGHT 377

Inside the building, he goes quickly up the steps. On one flight of steps, he passes one of the neighbors, Ron.

RON
Oh, Harry...

HARRY
(continuing past him)
Excuse me...I...

Ron turns and follows.

RON
(sternly)
Harry, it's important...we're all very upset.

Harry moves past them, without another word.

CUT TO:

378 INT. HARRY'S APARTMENT - NIGHT 378

He locks his door. He puts down the plastic pouch. He dials a number on his telephone.

HARRY
Extension 765.

OPERATOR (o.s.)
One moment.

MALE VOICE (o.s.)
The Director's office.

HARRY
I want to speak with the Director's assistant, Mr. Harrison. It's important; this is Mr. Caul.

VOICE (o.s.)
Moment.
(click)

Harry waits.

VOICE (o.s.)
(click)
I'm sorry, that's impossible now. May we get back to you?

(CONTINUED)

378 CONTINUED: 378

HARRY
I have to talk to him.

VOICE (o.s.)
Your name again?

HARRY
Caul.

VOICE (o.s.)
Spell it.

HARRY
Caul...C-A-U-L, Caul.

VOICE (o.s.)
I'm putting you on hold.

Harry waits, upset.

VOICE (o.s.)
Mr. Caul, we'll get right back to you.
(hangs up)

HARRY
But you don't have...

He realizes they've hung up. He drops the receiver into the cradle.

HARRY
...my number.

He is about to re-dial their number, when he pauses, and stops. He decides not to. He returns the telephone and regards it as an intruder. His paranoia rampant, he turns and looks at his door. He senses something and opens it without warning:

There are Bob and Ron, his neighbors, caught in the most primitive form of eavesdropping, their ears to the door.

HARRY
(smoldering)
What is this?

RON
We've got a bone to pick with you...we...

(CONTINUED)

379 CONTINUED: 379

BOB
Mrs. Evangelista told us that she thinks you own this building.

Harry rages, as though he is capable of great violence.

HARRY
And how did she find that out? By reading my mail, by listening on my telephone...by spying on me the way she found out that it was my birthday.

BOB
Harry, we...

HARRY
Get out of here! Get out! I'll evict you all! I'll tear the building doen.

He frightens them and slams the door.

379 CLOSE ON HARRY 379

He looks at his ragged, tense face in the mirror, rubbing the skin.

Then he HEARS the telephone ringing.

He walks into he main room slowly, all his attention focused on the telephone. The watches it ring for a while, then quickly, he answers it.

HARRY
How did you get this number?

MALE VOICE (o.s.)
It's in your dossier, Mr. Caul.

There's a pause, and then someone new takes the phone.

VOICE (o.s.)
Do you recognize my voice?

Harry shudders. It is Mark.

VOICE (o.s.)
Do you know who I am?

(CONTINUED)

379 CONTINUED: 379

HARRY
Yes.

MARK (o.s.)
You wanted to speak to Harrison. But he's gone now...you understand me?

HARRY
Yes.

MARK (o.s.)
Just listen to me. Leave it, Mr. Caul. Forget everything. It has nothing to do with you. All you can do is hurt yourself. Do you understand me?

HARRY
Yes.

MARK (o.s.)
I'll keep my eye on you...
(click)

Slowly, Harry hangs up.

CUT TO:

380 INT. HARRY'S ROOM - DAY 380

Harry sitting in the middle of his room on his wooden-backed chair, playing the saxophone to a record. After a moment, the telephone rings. He looks.

381 HARRY'S VIEW 381

The telephone.

382 MEDIUM VIEW 382

Harry rises; turns the volume down; answers it.

383 CLOSE ON HARRY 383

As soon as he listens; there is a click and then a dial tone.

CUT TO:

384 MEDIUM VIEW 384

Harry returns; turns up the music; and continues playing. The telephone rings. He stops and looks with horror at the phone. He answers it once again. The same click, and then silence. The record-changer has come to the end; and shuts itself off.

385 CLOSE ON HARRY 385

Staring at the telephone; moving it occasionally so as to look at it from different points of view. Then he takes a small pencil-screwdriver from his vest pocket and deftly with small, precise movements, loosens the screws that hold the case on the mechanism. In a moment, the insides of the instrument are exposed.

He dials a special number on the dial, and a 1ØØHz tone comes over the receiver. He checks the circuitry in what has now become an efficient ritual, tapping this, touching that, testing voltages here and there.

He unscrews the cap on the receiver, examining the microphone and speaker cartridges carefully. Satisfied that the instrument itself is clean, he traces the wires with his fingers, feeling the texture of the line down to the box on the wall. He opens and inspects the wall box.

Now he lifts the receiver, listening to the dial tone, and replaces it. He repeats this several times. He has not found the tap, if one exists.

386 CLOSE ANGLE ON HARRY 386

Glancing around the room; it could be anywhere.

387 HARRY'S POINT OF VIEW 387

Turning, looking at each corner, each apsect of the room.

388 MEDIUM VIEW 388

Calmly, he unscrews and removes the plates from each and every electric box. The light switches, the wall outlets, the lighting fixtures. He removes and inspects everything. He begins to turn the chairs upside down, slitting the soft material of their undersides, and feeling carefully underneath. He checks the couch and table as well.

(CONTINUED)

388 CONTINUED: 388

Then he begins to carry the furniture into the bed-room, stack them one on top of another, the tables, and then the chairs on top of them, and all the rest of the furniture, piece by piece.

389 CLOSER VIEW ON HARRY 389

He is nervous, more rattled, beginning to sweat, as he goes through another logical step, and cannot find the tap. He looks closer at the places where the furniture had been.

390 NEW VIEW 390

He gets on his hands and knees an begins to slowly roll the carpet, exposing the wood-grained floor. He carries the carpet roll with some difficulty, and stores it in the bedroom.

391 MOVING VIEW 391

Now he moves quickly around the room, taking every-thing down from the walls: the pictures, the little bric-a-brac, the curtains. Then he stops.

392 HARRY'S VIEW 392

A little plastic Madonna.

Harry moves to it, looking, a subtle smile moving over his face. He smashes it completely with his fist. But it's empty.

393 FULL VIEW ON THE ROOM 393

Harry turns, he is more confused, rattled. He circles the room, his sensitive fingers tracing the patterns on the walls, seeking the feel of hair-thin wires or some tell-tale hint.

394 MOVING VIEW ON HIS FINGERS 394

Gliding along the wallpaper.

395 NEW ANGLE 395

Harry exits the kitchen with a large bowl of steaming water, and a sponge. He moves to each of the four corners, and begins by splitting the wallpaper with a razor blade, and then soaking each with the saturated sponge. After soaking the fourth corner,

(CONTINUED)

395 CONTINUED: 395

he returns to he first, and begins to peel the paper away from the ceiling to the floor, exposing the bare wall underneath.

396 CLOSE ANGLE 396

He examines this carefully, but finds nothing. He continues soaking and peeling but there is nothing.

397 HIGH FULL ANGLE 397

Harry stands helplessly in his stripped down room. He gets on his hands and knees, prying the base-board apart from the wall, using a screwdriver.

At each phase, he realizes that something better must have been used, and he becomes more and more desperate until, in the privacy of his room, he begins to weep.

FADE OUT:

- THE END -

BUDGET FORM

Budget Form

FILM PRODUCTION BUDGET

DATE: ____________

PRODUCTION COMPANY | PRODUCTION TITLE | PRODUCTION NO.

EXECUTIVE PRODUCER | PRODUCER | DIRECTOR | PRODUCTION MANAGER

START DATE | FINISH DATE | SCRIPT DATED | SCRIPT PAGES | CREW DAILY PAY HRS.

ACCT NO.	DESCRIPTION	PAGE NO.	BUDGET	TOTALS
0000	Development	3		
1000	Story and Screenplay	4		
1100	Producers Unit	5		
1200	Directors Unit	6		
1300	Cast Unit	7		
1400	Travel and Living	8		
1900	Fringe Benefits and Payroll Taxes	9		
	TOTAL ABOVE THE LINE			
2000	Production Department	10		
2100	Extra Talent	11		
2200	Art Department	12		
2300	Set Construction	13		
2400	Set Dressing	14		
2500	Property	15		
2600	Picture Vehicles	16		
2700	Special Effects	17		
2800	Camera	18		
3000	Special Equipment	19		
3100	Sound	20		
3200	Grip	21		
3300	Lighting	22		
3400	Wardrobe	23		
3500	Makeup and Hair	24		
3600	Set Operations	25, 26		
3700	Site Rental	27		
3800	Stage Rental and Expense	28		
4000	Location Expense	29, 30		
4100	Second Unit	31, 32		
4200	Tests	33		
4300	Miniatures	34		
4400	Process	35		
4500	Animals	36		
4600	Transportation	37		
4700	Raw Stock and Laboratory	38		
4900	Fringe Benefits and Payroll Taxes	39		
	TOTAL BELOW THE LINE			

SAMPLE

FILM PRODUCTION BUDGET (Cont'd)

DATE: ____________________

PRODUCTION COMPANY ____________________ PRODUCTION TITLE ____________________ PRODUCTION NO. ____________________

ACCT NO.	DESCRIPTION	PAGE NO.	BUDGET	TOTALS
5000	Film Editing	40, 41		
5100	Music	42		
5200	Film Effects	43		
5300	Titles	44		
5400	Post Production Sound	45		
5500	Post Production Film	46		
5900	Fringe Benefits and Payroll Taxes	47		
	TOTAL POST PRODUCTION			
6000	Publicity	48		
6100	Insurance	49		
6200	General Expense	50		
6900	Fringe Benefits and Payroll Taxes	51		
	TOTAL OTHER COSTS			
	TOTAL DIRECT COSTS			
7500	Contingency	52		
7600	Completion Bond	52		
7700	Overhead	52		
7800	Interest	52		
	TOTAL NEGATIVE COSTS			
8000	Deferments	52		
	TOTAL NEGATIVE COSTS (Incl. Deferments)			

PRODUCTION DAYS

Rehearsal	
Studio	
Loc. Location	
Distant Location	
Holidays	
Travel	
Total Production Days	

BUDGET APPROVALS

____________________ Estimator

____________________ Exec. in Charge of Prod.

____________________ Producer

____________________ Production Manager

____________________ Date

PAGE NO. 3

PROD. NO. ____________ PROD. TITLE ____________ DATE: ____________

0000	DEVELOPMENT COSTS	SUBTOTALS		
ACCT. NO.	DESCRIPTION	A	B	C
	Story and Screenplay			
	Rights and Options			
	Drafts and Treatments			
	Typing			
	Script Duplication			
	Producer's Unit			
	Producer			
	Assoc. Producer			
	Secretary			
	Additional Hire			
	Director's Unit			
	Director			
	Secretary			
	Additional Hire			
	Budget Preparation			
	Script Breakdown, Production Board and			
	Budget Preparation Fee			
	Accounting			
	Legal			
	Incorporation			
	Contracts			
	Business License			
	Other			
	Office Overhead			
	Telephone and Telex			
	Answering Service			
	Telephone Installation Charge			
	Office Rent			
	Equipment/Furniture			
	Rental			
	Purchase			
	Data Processing			
	Supplies			
	Stationery			
	Postage			
	Transportation			
	Car Allowance			
	Gas, Oil			
	Additional Expenses			
	Miscellaneous			
	Fringe Benefits			
	SUBTOTALS			
	TOTAL ACCT 0000			

A - Fringeable/Taxable
B - Non-Fringeable/Taxable
C - Non-Taxable

PAGE NO. 4

PROD. NO. ____________ PROD. TITLE ____________ DATE: ____________

1000 STORY AND SCREENPLAY

ACCT. NO.	DESCRIPTION	LOCAL / ON LOC.	DAYS / WEEKS PREP	SHOOT	WRAP	TOTAL	RATE	SUBTOTALS A	B	C
10	Rights & Expenses	Local								
		On Loc.								
		Local								
		On Loc.								
20	Writers	Local								
		On Loc.								
		Local								
		On Loc.								
30	Script Writing	Local								
		On Loc.								
		Local								
		On Loc.								
40	Script Duplication	Local								
		On Loc.								
		Local								
		On Loc.								
50	Script Timing	Local								
		On Loc.								
		Local								
		On Loc.								
60	Secretary(ies)	Local								
		On Loc.								
		Local								
		On Loc.								
		Local								
		On Loc.								
70	Research, Technical, Screenings									
85	Additional Expenses									
95	Miscellaneous									
	SUBTOTALS									
	TOTAL ACCT 1000									

A - Fringeable/Taxable
B - Non-Fringeable/Taxable
C - Non-Taxable

PAGE NO. 5

PROD. NO. ____________ PROD. TITLE ____________ DATE: ____________

1100 PRODUCERS UNIT

ACCT. NO.	DESCRIPTION	LOCAL / ON LOC.	DAYS / WEEKS PREP	SHOOT	WRAP	TOTAL	RATE	SUBTOTALS A	B	C
01	Executive Producer(s)	Local								
		On Loc.								
		Local								
		On Loc.								
02	Producer(s)	Local								
		On Loc.								
		Local								
		On Loc.								
03	Associate Producer(s)	Local								
		On Loc.								
		Local								
		On Loc.								
60	Secretary(ies)	Local								
		On Loc.								
		Local								
		On Loc.								
		Local								
		On Loc.								
		Local								
		On Loc.								
		Local								
		On Loc.								
		Local								
		On Loc.								
		Local								
		On Loc.								
70	Research, Technical, Screenings									
80	Packaging Fee									
85	Additional Expenses									
95	Miscellaneous									
99	Loss, Damage, Repair									
	SUBTOTALS									
	TOTAL ACCT 1100									

A - Fringeable/Taxable
B - Non-Fringeable/Taxable
C - Non-Taxable

PAGE NO. 6

PROD. NO. ______ PROD. TITLE ______ DATE: ______

1200 DIRECTORS UNIT

ACCT. NO.	DESCRIPTION	LOCAL / ON LOC.	DAYS / WEEKS PREP	SHOOT	WRAP	TOTAL	RATE	SUBTOTALS A	B	C
01	Director	Local								
		On Loc.								
		Local								
		On Loc.								
02	Second Unit Director	Local								
		On Loc.								
		Local								
		On Loc.								
03	Choreographer	Local								
		On Loc.								
		Local								
		On Loc.								
04	Dialogue Director	Local								
		On Loc.								
		Local								
		On Loc.								
60	Secretary(ies)	Local								
		On Loc.								
		Local								
		On Loc.								
		Local								
		On Loc.								
		Local								
		On Loc.								
		Local								
		On Loc.								
70	Research, Technical, Screenings									
85	Additional Expenses									
95	Miscellaneous									
							SUBTOTALS			
							TOTAL ACCT 1200			

A - Fringeable/Taxable
B - Non-Fringeable/Taxable
C - Non-Taxable

PAGE NO. 7

PROD. NO. ______ PROD. TITLE ______ DATE: ______

1300	CAST UNIT				SUBTOTALS		
ACCT. NO.	DESCRIPTION	TIME	RATE	AMOUNT	A	B	C
01	Principal Players						
	(See Detail Page 7A)						
02	Supporting Players						
	(See Detail Page 7B)						
03	Day Players						
	(See Detail Page 7C)						
04	Stunt Coordinator						
05	Stunts (See Detail Page 7D)						
06	Looping						
07	Overtime						
08	Cast Expenses						
09	Casting Expenses						
10	Welfare Worker/Teacher						
11	Rehearsal Expenses						
85	Additional Expenses						
95	Miscellaneous						
	SUBTOTALS						
	TOTAL ACCT 1300						

A - Fringeable/Taxable
B - Non-Fringeable/Taxable
C - Non-Taxable

PAGE NO. 7A

PROD. NO. ____________ PROD. TITLE ____________ DATE: ____________

1301 PRINCIPAL PLAYERS						SUBTOTALS		
CAST NO.	CHARACTER	DAYS/WEEKS			RATE	A	B	C
		WORK	HOLD	TOTAL				
	SUBTOTALS							
	TOTAL DETAIL ACCT 1301							

A - Fringeable/Taxable
B - Non-Fringeable/Taxable
C - Non-Taxable

PAGE NO. 7B

PROD. NO. ______ PROD. TITLE ______ DATE: ______

1302 SUPPORTING PLAYERS						SUBTOTALS		
CAST NO.	CHARACTER	DAYS/WEEKS			RATE	A	B	C
		WORK	HOLD	TOTAL				
	SUBTOTALS							
	TOTAL DETAIL ACCT 1302							

A - Fringeable/Taxable
B - Non-Fringeable/Taxable
C - Non-Taxable

PAGE NO. 7C

PROD. NO. ____________ PROD. TITLE ____________ DATE: ____________

1303 DAY PLAYERS						SUBTOTALS		
CAST NO.	CHARACTER	DAYS			RATE	A	B	C
		WORK	HOLD	TOTAL				
	SUBTOTALS							
	TOTAL DETAIL ACCT 1303							

A - Fringeable/Taxable
B - Non-Fringeable/Taxable
C - Non-Taxable

PAGE NO. 7D

PROD. NO. ______ PROD. TITLE ______ DATE: ______

1305 STUNTS						SUBTOTALS		
CAST NO.	SCENE DESCRIPTION / NOS.	DAYS / WEEKS			RATE	A	B	C
		WORK	HOLD	TOTAL				
	SUBTOTALS							
	TOTAL DETAIL ACCT 1305							

SAMPLE

A - Fringeable/Taxable
B - Non-Fringeable/Taxable
C - Non-Taxable

LOCATION EXPENSE—DETAIL

PAGE NO. 8

PROD. NO. ____________ PROD. TITLE ____________ DATE: ____________

1400 TRAVEL AND LIVING—ABOVE-THE-LINE

		AIRFARES			LODGING (PER DIEM)			MEALS (PER DIEM)				
POSITION/NAME	DESTINATION (RT)	NO. FLIGHTS	RATE	SUBTOTAL	NO. DAYS	RATE	SUBTOTAL	NO. DAYS		RATE	SUBTOTAL	TOTALS
									B			
									L			
									D			
									B			
									L			
									D			
									B			
									L			
									D			
									B			
									L			
									D			
									B			
									L			
									D			
									B			
									L			
									D			
									B			
									L			
									D			
									B			
									L			
									D			
									B			
									L			
									D			
									B			
									L			
									D			
	SUBTOTALS	1401			1402			1403				
						TOTAL DETAIL ACCT 1400						

SAMPLE

A - Fringeable/Taxable
B - Non-Fringeable/Taxable
C - Non-Taxable

PAGE NO. 9

PROD. NO. ______ PROD. TITLE ______ DATE: ______

1900	FRINGE BENEFITS AND PAYROLL TAXES—ABOVE-THE-LINE				
ACCT NO.	DESCRIPTION	PAYROLL	PENSION	HEALTH & WELFARE	TOTALS
01	DGA $ ______	%	%	%	
02	PGA $ ______	%	%	%	
03	WGA $ ______	%	%	%	
04	SAG $ ______	%	%	%	
05	IATSE $ ______	%	%	%	
06	NABET $ ______	%	%	%	
07	OTHER $ ______	%	%	%	
10	or Allow				

SAMPLE

SUBTOTALS				

TOTAL ACCT 1900	

TOTAL COST ABOVE-THE-LINE	

PAGE NO. 10

PROD. NO. ____________ PROD. TITLE ____________ DATE: ____________

2000 PRODUCTION DEPARTMENT

NO.	DESCRIPTION	LOCAL/ ON LOC.	DAYS/WEEKS PREP	SHOOT	WRAP	TOTAL	RATE	SUBTOTALS A	B	C
01	Production Manager	Local								
		On Loc.								
		Local								
		On Loc.								
02	First Assistant Director	Local								
		On Loc.								
		Local								
		On Loc.								
03	Second Assistant Director	Local								
		On Loc.								
		Local								
		On Loc.								
05	Location Manager	Local								
		On Loc.								
		Local								
		On Loc.								
10	Production Accountant	Local								
		On Loc.								
15	Asst. to Production Accountant	Local								
		On Loc.								
20	D.G.A. Trainee	Local								
		On Loc.								
25	Production Assts.	Local								
		On Loc.								
		Local								
		On Loc.								
48	Interpreters	Local								
		On Loc.								
50	Script Supervisor	Local								
		On Loc.								
55	Production Office Coordinator	Local								
		On Loc.								
60	Production Secretary	Local								
		On Loc.								
	Additional Hire	Local								
		On Loc.								
80	Technical Advisor	Local								
		On Loc.								
85	Additional Expenses									
95	Miscellaneous									
97	Production Board/ Budget Prep.									
							SUBTOTALS			
							TOTAL ACCT 2000			

A - Fringeable/Taxable
B - Non-Fringeable/Taxable
C - Non-Taxable

PAGE NO. 11

PROD. NO. ____________ PROD. TITLE ____________ DATE: ____________

2100	EXTRA TALENT				SUBTOTALS		
ACCT. NO.	DESCRIPTION	TIME	RATE	AMT.	A	B	C
01	Extra Casting Fee						
03	Payroll Fee						
05	Extra Casting Expenses						
10	Welfare Workers/Teachers						
20	Extras & Stand-ins						
	(Detail Following Page 11A)						
35	Dancers/Swimmers						
43	Music Contractor						
45	Sideline Musicians						
48	Interviews/Fittings						
60	Extras Mileage Allowance (See Detail Page 11A)						
	Buses (See Transportation Acct 4603)						
	Meals (See Catering Acct 3620)						
70	Rehearsal Expenses						
	Additional Hire						
85	Additional Expenses						
95	Miscellaneous						
99	Loss, Damage, Repair						
	SUBTOTALS						
	TOTAL ACCT 2100						

A - Fringeable/Taxable
B - Non-Fringeable/Taxable
C - Non-Taxable

PAGE NO. 11A

PROD. NO. ______ PROD. TITLE ______ DATE: ______

2100 EXTRA TALENT—DETAIL

DAY NO.	BREAK-DOWN PAGE	SCENE NO.	SCENE NAME/DESCRIPTION	A–GENERAL B–STAND-INS			C–SILENT BITS D–SPECIAL EXTRAS			O.T.	MILEAGE			SUBTOTALS	
				NO.	RATE	AMOUNT	NO.	RATE	AMOUNT	ADJ.	NO.	RATE	AMOUNT	A	B
														SUBTOTALS	
														TOTAL DETAIL ACCT 2100	

A - Fringeable/Taxable
B - Non-Fringeable/Taxable
C - Non-Taxable

PAGE NO. 12

PROD. NO. ______ PROD. TITLE ______ DATE: ______

2200 ART DEPARTMENT

ACCT. NO.	DESCRIPTION	LOCAL/ ON LOC.	DAYS/WEEKS PREP	SHOOT	WRAP	TOTAL	RATE	SUBTOTALS A	B	C
01	Production Designer	Local								
		On Loc.								
02	Art Director	Local								
		On Loc.								
03	Assistant Art Director	Local								
		On Loc.								
04	Set Designer	Local								
		On Loc.								
		Local								
		On Loc.								
05	Draftsman	Local								
		On Loc.								
		Local								
		On Loc.								
09	Sketch Artist	Local								
		On Loc.								
10	Set Model Builders	Local								
		On Loc.								
15	Set Estimator	Local								
		On Loc.								
	Additional Hire	Local								
		On Loc.								
		Local								
		On Loc.								
		Local								
		On Loc.								
30	Rentals									
40	Purchases									
70	Research									
85	Additional Expense									
95	Miscellaneous									
99	Loss, Damage, Repair									
							SUBTOTALS			
							TOTAL ACCT 2200			

A - Fringeable/Taxable
B - Non-Fringeable/Taxable
C - Non-Taxable

PAGE NO. 13

PROD. NO. ____________ PROD. TITLE ____________ DATE: ____________

2300 SET CONSTRUCTION

ACCT. NO.	DESCRIPTION	NO.	LOCAL / ON LOC.	DAYS/WEEKS PREP	SHOOT	WRAP	TOTAL	RATE	SUBTOTALS A	B	C
01	Construction Coordinator		Local								
			On Loc.								
05	Construction Foreman		Local								
			On Loc.								
	Labor	NO.									
11	Painters		Local								
			On Loc.								
12	Scenic Artists		Local								
			On Loc.								
13	Carpenters		Local								
			On Loc.								
14	Propmakers		Local								
			On Loc.								
15	Laborers		Local								
			On Loc.								
16	Plumbers		Local								
			On Loc.								
17	Electrical Fixtures Man		Local								
			On Loc.								
18	Plasterers		Local								
			On Loc.								
			Local								
			On Loc.								
	Additional Hire		Local								
			On Loc.								
20	Set Construction Materials (See 13A)										
30	Set Equipment/Rentals (See 13B)										
35	Backings (See 13A)										
40	Set Equipment/Purchases (See 13B)										
55	Set Striking Maintenance (See 13A)										
	Rigging (See 13A)										
	Greens (See Set Dressing Acct 2410)										
75	Pickup and Delivery										
85	Additional Expense										
95	Miscellaneous										
99	Loss, Damage, Repair										
								SUBTOTALS			
								TOTAL ACCT 2300			

A - Fringeable/Taxable
B - Non-Fringeable/Taxable
C - Non-Taxable

PAGE NO. 13A

PROD. NO. ______________ PROD. TITLE ______________ DATE: ______________

2300 SET CONSTRUCTION DETAIL

SET NO.	SCENE NAME/NO. DESCRIPTION	LABOR	MATERIALS	BACKINGS	SET RIGGING	SET STRIKING	SUBTOTALS A	B	C
	SUBTOTALS								
	TOTAL DETAIL ACCT 2300								

A - Fringeable/Taxable
B - Non-Fringeable/Taxable
C - Non-Taxable

PAGE NO. 14

PROD. NO. ____________ PROD. TITLE ____________ DATE: ____________

2400 SET DRESSING

ACCT. NO.	DESCRIPTION	LOCAL/ ON LOC.	DAYS/WEEKS PREP	SHOOT	WRAP	TOTAL	RATE	SUBTOTALS A	B	C
01	Set Decorator	Local								
		On Loc.								
05	Swing Gang—Leadman	Local								
		On Loc.								
06	Swing Gang—Second	Local								
		On Loc.								
07	Swing Gang—Local	Local								
		On Loc.								
10	Greensman	Local								
		On Loc.								
12	Draperer	Local								
		On Loc.								
15	Standby Painter	Local								
		On Loc.								
	Additional Hire	Local								
		On Loc.								
		Local								
		On Loc.								
20	Set Dressing Manufactured—Labor									
25	Drapery and Upholstery—Labor									
30	Rentals									
	Set Dressing (See Detail Page 14A)									
	Paint Box									
	Greens									
40	Purchases									
	Set Dressing (See Detail Page 14A)									
	Expendables									
	Paint									
	Greens									
75	Delivery and Pickup Charges									
85	Additional Expense									
95	Miscellaneous									
99	Loss, Damage, Repair									
							SUBTOTALS			
							TOTAL ACCT 2400			

A - Fringeable/Taxable
B - Non-Fringeable/Taxable
C - Non-Taxable

PAGE NO. 14A

PROD. NO. ____________ PROD. TITLE ____________ DATE: ____________

ACCTS 2430 & 2440 SET DRESSING—DETAIL

SET NO.	SCENE NAME/NO. DESCRIPTION	ITEM QTY	ITEM DESCRIPTION	RENTALS TIME	RENTALS RATE	RENTALS AMOUNT	PURCHASES AMOUNT	✓
SUBTOTALS								
TOTAL DETAIL ACCTS 2430 & 2440								

SAMPLE

A - Fringeable/Taxable
B - Non-Fringeable/Taxable
C - Non-Taxable
✓ - Recoupable

PAGE NO. 15

PROD. NO. ____________ PROD. TITLE ____________ DATE: ____________

2500 PROP DEPARTMENT										
ACCT. NO.	DESCRIPTION	LOCAL / ON LOC.	DAYS / WEEKS PREP	SHOOT	WRAP	TOTAL	RATE	SUBTOTALS A	B	C
01	Propmaster	Local								
		On Loc.								
		Local								
		On Loc.								
02	Asst. Propmaster	Local								
		On Loc.								
		Local								
		On Loc.								
03	Add'l. Asst. Propmaster	Local								
		On Loc.								
		Local								
		On Loc.								
		Local								
		On Loc.								
	Additional Hire	Local								
		On Loc.								
		Local								
		On Loc.								
		Local								
		On Loc.								
		Local								
		On Loc.								
		Local								
		On Loc.								
		Local								
		On Loc.								
30	Prop Rentals (See Detail Page 15A)									
	Video Playback System									
	Prop Box									
40	Prop Purchases (See Detail Page 15A)									
50	Props Manufactured — Labor									
55	Props Manufactured — Materials									
65	Permits (Guns and Ammo.)									
75	Pickup and Delivery									
85	Additional Expense									
95	Miscellaneous									
99	Loss, Damage, Repair									
							SUBTOTALS			
							TOTAL ACCT 2500			

SAMPLE

A - Fringeable/Taxable
B - Non-Fringeable/Taxable
C - Non-Taxable

PAGE NO. 15A

PROD. NO. ________ PROD. TITLE ________ DATE: ________

ACCTS 2530 & 2540 PROPS—DETAIL

SET NO.	SCENE NAME/NO. DESCRIPTION	ITEM QTY	ITEM DESCRIPTION	RENTALS TIME	RENTALS RATE	RENTALS AMOUNT	PURCHASES AMOUNT	✓
			SUBTOTALS					
			TOTAL DETAIL ACCTS 2530 & 2540					

SAMPLE

A - Fringeable/Taxable
B - Non-Fringeable/Taxable
C - Non-Taxable
✓ - Recoupable

PAGE NO. 16

PROD. NO. ______ PROD. TITLE ______ DATE: ______

2600	PICTURE VEHICLES	SUBTOTALS		
ACCT. NO.	DESCRIPTION	A	B	C
01	Vehicle Drivers (Non-Teamsters/Vehicle's owner			
	or representative)			
02				
	Transportation Allowance (See Location Acct 4005)			
30	Rental (See Detail Page 16A)			
	Cars/Trucks			
	Motorcycles			
	Planes/Helicopters			
	Trains			
	Boats			
40	Purchases (See Detail Page 16A)			
	Cars/Trucks			
	Motorcycles			
	Planes/Helicopters			
	Trains			
	Boats			
	Car Carrier (See Transportation Acct No. 4600)			
45	Special Vehicle Use Permit (Check local regulations)			
48	Vehicle Alterations, Modifications, and Repairs			
	Gas and Oil (See Transportation Acct 4650)			
60	Permits, Parking, Tolls, Fees, etc. (See Transportation Acct 4669)			
65	Rigging Maintenance			
70	Storage			
72	Security			
75	Shop			
	Insurance (See Insurance Acct No. 6100)			
85	Additional Expenses			
95	Miscellaneous			
99	Loss, Damage, Repair			
	SUBTOTALS			
	TOTAL ACCT 2600			

A - Fringeable/Taxable C - Non-Taxable
B - Non-Fringeable/Taxable

PAGE NO. 16A

PROD. NO. ______________ PROD. TITLE ______________ DATE: ______________

ACCTS 2630 & 2640 PICTURE VEHICLES—DETAIL

SET	SCENE NAME/NO.	VEHICLES		RENTAL			PURCHASES	✓
NO.	DESCRIPTION	QTY	DESCRIPTION	TIME	RATE	AMOUNT	AMOUNT	
					SUBTOTALS			
					TOTAL DETAIL ACCTS 2630 & 2640			

A - Fringeable/Taxable
B - Non-Fringeable/Taxable
C - Non-Taxable
✓ - Recoupable

PAGE NO. 17

PROD. NO. ____________ PROD. TITLE ____________ DATE: ____________

2700 SPECIAL EFFECTS DEPARTMENT

ACCT. NO.	DESCRIPTION	LOCAL / ON LOC.	DAYS/WEEKS PREP	SHOOT	WRAP	TOTAL	RATE	SUBTOTALS A	B	C
01	Special Effects Foreman	Local								
		On Loc.								
		Local								
		On Loc.								
02	Assistant Spec. Eff. Men	Local								
		On Loc.								
		Local								
		On Loc.								
	Additional Hire	Local								
		On Loc.								
		Local								
		On Loc.								
05	Rigging	Local								
		On Loc.								
		Local								
		On Loc.								
06	Striking	Local								
		On Loc.								
30	Equipment Rentals									
	Wind									
	Rain									
	Snow									
	Fog									
	Fire Hose Wet Downs									
	Box Rental (Water Wagon—See Transportation Acct 4630)									
40	Equipment Purchases									
	Explosives, Breakaways, etc.									
50	Manufacturing—Labor									
55	Manufacturing—Materials									
65	Permits (Explosives, Fire, etc.)									
79	Other Charges, Permits, Fees, etc.									
85	Additional Expense									
95	Miscellaneous									
99	Loss, Damage, Repair									
	SUBTOTALS									
	TOTAL ACCT 2700									

A - Fringeable/Taxable
B - Non-Fringeable/Taxable
C - Non-Taxable

PAGE NO. 17A

PROD. NO. ____________ PROD. TITLE ____________ DATE: ____________

ACCTS 2730 & 2740 SPECIAL EFFECTS—DETAIL

SET NO.	SCENE NAME/NO. DESCRIPTION	ITEM QTY	ITEM DESCRIPTION	RENTALS TIME	RENTALS RATE	RENTALS AMOUNT	PURCHASES AMOUNT	✓
						SUBTOTALS		
						TOTAL DETAIL ACCTS 2730 & 2740		

A - Fringeable/Taxable
B - Non-Fringeable/Taxable
C - Non-Taxable
✓ - Recoupable

PAGE NO. 18

PROD. NO. ______ PROD. TITLE ______ DATE: ______

2800 CAMERA DEPARTMENT

ACCT. NO.	DESCRIPTION	LOCAL / ON LOC.	DAYS / WEEKS PREP	SHOOT	WRAP	TOTAL	RATE	SUBTOTALS A	B	C
01	Director of Photography	Local								
		On Loc.								
		Local								
		On Loc.								
		Local								
		On Loc.								
02	Camera Operator	Local								
		On Loc.								
03	Additional Camera Operator	Local								
		On Loc.								
		Local								
		On Loc.								
05	1st Assistant Cameraman	Local								
		On Loc.								
		Local								
		On Loc.								
10	2nd Assistant Cameraman	Local								
		On Loc.								
12	Add'l 2nd Ass't Cameraman	Local								
		On Loc.								
	Still Photographer (See Publicity, Acct 6000)	Local								
		On Loc.								
15	Special Camera Operator	Local								
		On Loc.								
	Additional Hire	Local								
		On Loc.								
30	Rentals									
	First Camera System									
	Second Camera System									
	Through-The-Lens Video System									
	Other									
40	Purchases									
85	Additional Expense									
95	Miscellaneous									
99	Loss, Damage, Repair									
							SUBTOTALS			
							TOTAL ACCT 2800			

A - Fringeable/Taxable
B - Non-Fringeable/Taxable
C - Non-Taxable

PAGE NO. 19

PROD. NO. ______ PROD. TITLE ______ DATE: ______

3000	SPECIAL EQUIPMENT							
ACCT NO.	DESCRIPTION / SCENE NO.	RENTAL	PURCHASE	LABOR	FUEL/ MATERIALS	PICK-UP DELIVERY	OTHER	TOTAL
01	Helicopter							
05	Plane							
10	Train							
15	Boat							
20	Underwater Equipment							
25	Industrial Crane							
31	Scissors Lift							
35	Cherry Picker							
	Hand Held Camera							
	(See Camera Dept. Acct 2800)							
42	Wind Machine							
45	Low Boy							
-	Additional Equipment							
							SUBTOTAL	

		TIME	RATE	AMOUNT	SUBTOTALS A	SUBTOTALS B	SUBTOTALS C
	Per Diem (List on Page 30C)						
	Travel (List on Page 30C)						
85	Additional Expenses						
95	Miscellaneous						
99	Loss, Damage, Repair						
				SUBTOTALS			
				TOTAL ACCT 3000			

SAMPLE

A - Fringeable/Taxable
B - Non-Fringeable/Taxable
C - Non-Taxable

PAGE NO. 20

PROD. NO. ______ PROD. TITLE ______ DATE: ______

3100 SOUND DEPARTMENT

ACCT. NO.	DESCRIPTION	LOCAL / ON LOC.	DAYS/WEEKS PREP	SHOOT	WRAP	TOTAL	RATE	SUBTOTALS A	B	C
01	Mixer	Local								
		On Loc.								
		Local								
		On Loc.								
02	Mike Boom Operator	Local								
		On Loc.								
		Local								
		On Loc.								
03	Cable Puller	Local								
		On Loc.								
		Local								
		On Loc.								
04	Playback Operator	Local								
		On Loc.								
		Local								
		On Loc.								
05	P.A. Operator	Local								
		On Loc.								
		Local								
		On Loc.								
	Additional Hire	Local								
		On Loc.								
		Local								
		On Loc.								
06	Daily Transfers (Labor)	Local								
		On Loc.								
30	Equipment Rentals									
	Basic Sound Package									
	Radio Mikes									
	Walkie-Talkies									
	Playback									
	P.A.									
	Special Boom									
	Bullhorn									
40	Equipment Purchases									
	1/4" Audiotape—Batteries (See Prod. Rawstock Acct. 4700)									
85	Additional Expense									
95	Miscellaneous									
99	Loss, Damage, Repair									
	SUBTOTALS									
	TOTAL ACCT 3100									

A - Fringeable/Taxable
B - Non-Fringeable/Taxable
C - Non-Taxable

PAGE NO. 21

PROD. NO. ____ PROD. TITLE ____ DATE: ____

3200 GRIP DEPARTMENT

ACCT. NO.	DESCRIPTION	LOCAL / ON LOC.	DAYS/WEEKS PREP	SHOOT	WRAP	TOTAL	RATE	SUBTOTALS A	B	C
01	Key Grip	Local								
		On Loc.								
		Local								
		On Loc.								
02	2nd Company Grip	Local								
		On Loc.								
		Local								
		On Loc.								
03	Dolly Grip	Local								
		On Loc.								
04	Crane Grip	Local								
		On Loc.								
05	Company Grip	Local								
		On Loc.								
		Local								
		On Loc.								
		Local								
		On Loc.								
	Additional Hire	Local								
		On Loc.								
		Local								
		On Loc.								
06	Rigging & Striking (See Also Acct 2300)	Local								
		On Loc.								
		Local								
		On Loc.								
30	Rentals									
	Dolly									
	Dolly Track									
	Crane									
	Grip Package									
40	Purchases									
	Gels									
85	Additional Expense									
95	Miscellaneous									
99	Loss, Damage, Repair									
							SUBTOTALS			
							TOTAL ACCT 3200			

A - Fringeable/Taxable
B - Non-Fringeable/Taxable
C - Non-Taxable

PAGE NO. 22

PROD. NO. ________ PROD. TITLE ________ DATE: ________

3300 LIGHTING DEPARTMENT

ACCT. NO.	DESCRIPTION	LOCAL/ ON LOC.	DAYS/WEEKS PREP	SHOOT	WRAP	TOTAL	RATE	SUBTOTALS A	B	C
01	Gaffer	Local								
		On Loc.								
03	Best Boy	Local								
		On Loc.								
04	Generator Operator	Local								
		On Loc.								
05	Electricians	Local								
		On Loc.								
	Additional Hire	Local								
		On Loc.								
		Local								
		On Loc.								
06	Rigging & Striking (See Also Acct 2300)	Local								
		On Loc.								
		Local								
		On Loc.								
		Local								
		On Loc.								
30	Equipment Rentals									
	Generator (A.C./D.C. Power)									
	Equipment Package									
	Lamps, Arc Lights (D.C. Power)									
	Dimmers/Cables, Connectors									
	H.M.I. Lights (A.C. Power)									
	H.M.I. Bulb Time									
	Box Rental									
	Additional Equipment									
40	Equipment Purchases									
	Globes and Carbons									
	Fuses, Plugs, Tapes, Other Expendables									
	Generator Gas & Oil									
85	Additional Expense									
95	Miscellaneous									
99	Loss, Damage, Repair									
							SUBTOTALS			
							TOTAL ACCT 3300			

A - Fringeable/Taxable
B - Non-Fringeable/Taxable
C - Non-Taxable

PAGE NO. 23

PROD. NO. ____________ PROD. TITLE ____________ DATE: ____________

3400 WARDROBE DEPARTMENT

ACCT. NO.	DESCRIPTION	LOCAL / ON LOC.	DAYS / WEEKS PREP	SHOOT	WRAP	TOTAL	RATE	SUBTOTALS A	B	C
01	Costume Designer	Local								
		On Loc.								
02	Asst. To Costume Designer	Local								
		On Loc.								
		Local								
		On Loc.								
05	Women's Costumer	Local								
		On Loc.								
06	Women's Costumer—Set	Local								
		On Loc.								
		Local								
		On Loc.								
		Local								
		On Loc.								
07	Men's Costumer	Local								
		On Loc.								
08	Men's Costumer—Set	Local								
		On Loc.								
09	Tailor	Local								
		On Loc.								
10	Seamstress	Local								
		On Loc.								
		Local								
		On Loc.								
	Additional Hire	Local								
		On Loc.								
30	Rentals (See Wardrobe Detail Page 23A)									
	Box Rental									
40	Purchases (See Wardrobe Detail Page 23A)									
	Manufacturing									
	Equipment									
	Alteration Material									
45	Dry Cleaning and Laundry									
85	Additional Expense									
95	Miscellaneous									
99	Loss, Damage, Repair									
							SUBTOTALS			
							TOTAL ACCT 3400			

A - Fringeable/Taxable
B - Non-Fringeable/Taxable
C - Non-Taxable

PAGE NO. 23A

PROD. NO. ____________ PROD. TITLE ____________ DATE: ____________

ACCTS 3430 & 3440 WARDROBE—DETAIL

CAST	SCENE NAME / NO.	ITEM		RENTALS			PURCHASES	✓
NO.	CHARACTER	QTY	DESCRIPTION	TIME	RATE	AMOUNT	AMOUNT	
					SUBTOTALS			
					TOTAL DETAIL ACCTS 3430 & 3440			

SAMPLE

A - Fringeable/Taxable
B - Non-Fringeable/Taxable
C - Non-Taxable
✓ - Recoupable

PAGE NO. 24

PROD. NO. ______ PROD. TITLE ______ DATE: ______

3500 MAKEUP and HAIRDRESSING DEPARTMENT

ACCT. NO.	DESCRIPTION	LOCAL / ON LOC.	DAYS / WEEKS PREP	SHOOT	WRAP	TOTAL	RATE	SUBTOTALS A	B	C
01	1st Makeup Artist	Local								
		On Loc.								
02	2nd Makeup Artist	Local								
		On Loc.								
03	Makeup Assistant	Local								
		On Loc.								
		Local								
		On Loc.								
05	Body Makeup	Local								
		On Loc.								
		Local								
		On Loc.								
	Additional Hire	Local								
		On Loc.								
		Local								
		On Loc.								
10	1st Hairstylist	Local								
		On Loc.								
11	2nd Hairstylist	Local								
		On Loc.								
12	Hairstylist Asst.	Local								
		On Loc.								
	Additional Hire	Local								
		On Loc.								
		Local								
		On Loc.								
30	Rentals									
	Equipment, Tables, Chairs, Mirrors									
	Box Rentals									
40	Purchases									
	Lights, Bulbs									
	Makeup Supplies									
	Hairdressing Supplies									
	Wigs and Hairpieces									
85	Additional Expense									
95	Miscellaneous									
99	Loss, Damage, Repair									
	SUBTOTALS									
	TOTAL ACCT 3500									

SAMPLE

A - Fringeable/Taxable
B - Non-Fringeable/Taxable
C - Non-Taxable

PAGE NO. 24A

PROD. NO. ____________ PROD. TITLE ____________ DATE: ____________

ACCTS 3530 & 3540 MAKEUP AND HAIRDRESSING—DETAIL

CAST	SCENE NAME / NO.	ITEM		RENTALS			PURCHASES	
NO.	CHARACTER	QTY	DESCRIPTION	TIME	RATE	AMOUNT	AMOUNT	✓
					SUBTOTALS			
					TOTAL DETAIL ACCTS 3530 & 3540			

A - Fringeable/Taxable
B - Non-Fringeable/Taxable
C - Non-Taxable
✓ - Recoupable

PAGE NO. 25

PROD. NO. ______ PROD. TITLE ______ DATE: ______

3600 SET OPERATIONS

ACCT. NO.	DESCRIPTION	LOCAL / ON LOC.	DAYS / WEEKS PREP	SHOOT	WRAP	TOTAL	RATE	SUBTOTALS A	B	C
01	Caterer/Driver	Local								
		On Loc.								
02	Caterer/Asst.	Local								
		On Loc.								
04	Craft Service	Local								
		On Loc.								
05	First Aid / Nurse	Local								
		On Loc.								
06	Doctor	Local								
		On Loc.								
07	Police	Local								
		On Loc.								
08	Firemen	Local								
		On Loc.								
09	Guards/ Watchmen	Local								
		On Loc.								
	Additional Hire	Local								
		On Loc.								
10	Police Vehicle Expense									
11	Ambulance									
15	Fire Equipment									
20	Catering Costs (No. People x No. Days x Rate)									
	Coffee, Rolls, etc.									
	Breakfast									
	Lunch									
	Dinner									
	Soft Drinks, etc.									
	Tables, Chairs									
	Taxes									
	Caterer - Mileage (Travel & Living See Location Acct 4000)									
	Hotel & Restaurant Gratuities									
	SUBTOTALS THIS PAGE									
	CONTINUED ON NEXT PAGE									

A - Fringeable/Taxable
B - Non-Fringeable/Taxable
C - Non-Taxable

PAGE NO. 26

PROD. NO. ______ PROD. TITLE ______ DATE: ______

3600	SET OPERATIONS—(CONT'D)	SUBTOTALS		
ACCT. NO.	DESCRIPTION	A	B	C
25	Courtesy Payments			
26	Weather Service			
27	Portable Toilets (Weeks x Rate)			
29	Transportation Fee			
30	Rentals (Weeks x Rate)			
	Craftservice Box			
	Dolly, Dolly Track, Crane (See Grip Dept. Acct 3200)			
	Grip Package & Grip Box (See Grip Dept. Acct 3200)			
	Camera Platform, Planes, Helicopters, Trains, Boats, etc.			
	(See Special Equipment Acct 3000)			
	Paint Box (See Set Dressing Dept. Acct 2400)			
	Greens (See Set Dressing Dept. Acct 2400)			
40	Purchases (Weeks x Rate)			
	Craftservice			
	Greens (See Set Dressing Acct 2400)			
	Paint (See Set Dressing Acct 2400)			
85	Additional Expenses			
95	Miscellaneous			
99	Loss, Damage, Repair			
	SUBTOTALS FROM PREVIOUS PAGE			
	SUBTOTALS THIS PAGE			
	TOTAL ACCT 3600			

A - Fringeable/Taxable
B - Non-Fringeable/Taxable
C - Non-Taxable

PAGE NO. 27

PROD. NO. ______ PROD. TITLE ______ DATE: ______

3700	LOCAL SITE RENTAL EXPENSE	SUBTOTALS		
ACCT. NO.	DESCRIPTION	A	B	C
01	Site Contact/Broker			
	Location Manager (See Acct 2000)			
03	Site Rental (See Detail Page 27A)			
04	Survey Costs — Scouting			
	Mileage			
	Gas/Oil			
08	Gratuities			
09	Meals			
17	Courtesy Payments (See Also Accts 6204 and 3625)			
25	Permits, Fees, etc. (See Detail Page 27A)			
27	Parking (Crew and Equipment)			
	Medical, Police, Fireman, etc. (See Set Operations Acct 3600)			
32	Messenger Service			
35	Janitorial			
	Additional Hire			
85	Additional Expenses			
95	Miscellaneous			
99	Loss, Damage, Repair			
	SUBTOTALS			
	TOTAL ACCT 3700			

A - Fringeable/Taxable
B - Non-Fringeable/Taxable
C - Non-Taxable

PAGE NO. 27A

PROD. NO. ______ PROD. TITLE ______ DATE: ______

3703 LOCAL SITE RENTAL—DETAIL

SET NO.	SCENE NAME/NO.	PREP			SHOOT			STRIKE			PERMITS, FEES	TOTALS
		TIME	RATE	AMT.	TIME	RATE	AMT.	TIME	RATE	AMT.		
	SUBTOTALS											
								TOTAL DETAIL ACCT 3703				

A - Fringeable/Taxable
B - Non-Fringeable/Taxable
C - Non-Taxable

PAGE NO. 28

PROD. NO. ____________ PROD. TITLE ____________ DATE: ____________

3800	STAGE RENTAL AND EXPENSE				SUBTOTALS		
ACCT. NO.	DESCRIPTION	TIME	RATE	AMT.	A	B	C
01	Guards						
02	Lot Man (Local 40)						
03	Utility Person						
	Additional Hire						
05	Power						
06	Equipment Package						
	Grip						
	Electrical						
	Cherry Picker						
	Forklift, etc.						
30	Rental						
	(See Detail Page 28A)						
65	Office Rental						
70	Telephone						
85	Additional Expenses						
95	Miscellaneous						
99	Loss, Damage, Repair						
	SUBTOTALS						
	TOTAL ACCT 3800						

A - Fringeable/Taxable
B - Non-Fringeable/Taxable
C - Non-Taxable

PAGE NO. 28A

PROD. NO. ______ PROD. TITLE ______ DATE: ______

3830 STAGE RENTAL—DETAIL

		CONSTRUCTION		REHEARSAL		HOLD		TEST		SHOOT		STRIKE		TOTAL	
SET NO.	SCENE NAME/NUMBER	TIME	RATE	TIME	RATE	TIME	RATE	TIME	RATE	TIME	RATE	TIME	RATE	TIME	AMOUNT
	SUBTOTALS														
													TOTAL DETAIL ACCT 3830		

A - Fringeable/Taxable
B - Non-Fringeable/Taxable
C - Non-Taxable

PAGE NO. 29

PROD. NO. ____ PROD. TITLE ____ DATE: ____

4000	LOCATION EXPENSE				SUBTOTALS		
ACCT. NO.	DESCRIPTION	TIME	RATE	AMT.	A	B	C
01	Location Contact/Broker						
	Location Mgr. (See Acct 2000)						
	Interpreters (See Acct 2000)						
02	Location Site Rental (See Detail 30A)						
03	Permits						
04	Scouting Costs (See Detail 30B)						
	Travel and Living (See Detail Page 30B)						
	Local Contact						
	Vehicle Rentals						
	Additional Expenses						
05	Transportation to Location						
	(See Detail 30C)						
06	Flight Insurance						
07	Passports, Visas and Work Permits						
08	Travel Gratuities & Excess Baggage						
09	Travel and Living (See Detail Page 30C)						
	Travel						
	Lodging						
	Meals						
	Catering Costs						
	(See Set Operations Acct 3600)						
10	Shipping Costs (Also See Acct 6203)						
	Custom and Brokerage Fees						
	Export Taxes						
	Equipment Shipment						
	Loading and Unloading Crates						
	Packing/Crating, Labor & Materials						
	Film Shipments						
	Air Freight						
	Airport Pickups & Deliveries						
	SUBTOTALS						
	CONTINUED ON NEXT PAGE						

A - Fringeable/Taxable C - Non-Taxable
B - Non-Fringeable/Taxable

PAGE NO. 30

PROD. NO. ______ PROD. TITLE ______ DATE: ______

4000	LOCATION EXPENSE—(Cont'd)	SUBTOTALS		
ACCT. NO.	DESCRIPTION	A	B	C
11	Postage (Also See Acct 6230)			
12	Office Supplies (Also See Acct 6230)			
13	Office Rental (Also See Acct 6220)			
14	Office Equipment and Furniture Rental (Also See Acct 6220)			
15	Special Equipment			
16	Telephone and Telegraph (Also See Acct 6220)			
	Installation Charges			
17	Courtesy Payments (Also See Acct 6204 & 3625)			
18	Government Censors			
19	Location Weather Service			
22	Local Projection Service			
25	Permits (Props and Special Effects)			
26	Storage/Working Space Rental			
	Wardrobe			
	Makeup/Hair			
	Carpentry			
	Prop			
	Set Dressing			
	Special Effects			
	General Storage			
	Vehicles (See Transportation Acct 4600)			
27	Parking			
	Location Medical, Police, Firemen			
	Watchmen (See Set Operations Acct 3600)			
28	Messenger Service			
29	Janitorial/Cleaning			
35	Hotel and Restaurant Gratuities			
85	Additional Expenses			
95	Miscellaneous			
99	Loss, Damage, Repair			
	SUBTOTALS FROM PREVIOUS PAGE			
	SUBTOTALS THIS PAGE			
	TOTAL ACCT 4000			

A - Fringeable/Taxable
B - Non-Fringeable/Taxable
C - Non-Taxable

PAGE NO. 30A

PROD. NO. ______ PROD. TITLE ______ DATE: ______

4002 LOCATION SITE RENTAL—DETAIL

SET NO.	SCENE NAME/NO.	PREP			SHOOT			STRIKE			PERMITS, FEES	TOTALS
		TIME	RATE	AMT.	TIME	RATE	AMT.	TIME	RATE	AMT.		
	SUBTOTALS											
									TOTAL DETAIL ACCT 4002			

A - Fringeable/Taxable
B - Non-Fringeable/Taxable
C - Non-Taxable

LOCATION EXPENSE—DETAIL

PAGE NO. 30B

PROD. NO. ____________ PROD. TITLE ____________ DATE: ____________

4004 SCOUTING COSTS — TRAVEL AND LIVING

POSITION/NAME	DESTINATION (RT)	AIRFARES			LODGING (PER DIEM)			MEALS (PER DIEM)				TOTALS
		NO. FLIGHTS	RATE	SUBTOTAL	NO. DAYS	RATE	SUBTOTAL	NO. DAYS		RATE	SUBTOTAL	
									B			
									L			
									D			
									B			
									L			
									D			
									B			
									L			
									D			
									B			
									L			
									D			
									B			
									L			
									D			
									B			
									L			
									D			
									B			
									L			
									D			
									B			
									L			
									D			
									B			
									L			
									D			
									B			
									L			
									D			
			SUBTOTALS									
								TOTAL DETAIL ACCT 4004				

A - Fringeable/Taxable
B - Non-Fringeable/Taxable
C - Non-Taxable

LOCATION EXPENSE—DETAIL

PAGE NO. 30C

PROD. NO. ________ PROD. TITLE ________ DATE: ________

4005 ON LOCATION—TRAVEL AND LIVING

		AIRFARES			LODGING (PER DIEM)			MEALS (PER DIEM)				
POSITION/NAME	DESTINATION (RT)	NO. FLIGHTS	RATE	SUBTOTAL	NO. DAYS	RATE	SUBTOTAL	NO. DAYS		RATE	SUBTOTAL	TOTALS
									B			
									L			
									D			
									B			
									L			
									D			
									B			
									L			
									D			
									B			
									L			
									D			
									B			
									L			
									D			
									B			
									L			
									D			
									B			
									L			
									D			
									B			
									L			
									D			
									B			
									L			
									D			
									B			
									L			
									D			
			SUBTOTALS									
								TOTAL DETAIL ACCT 4005				

A - Fringeable/Taxable
B - Non-Fringeable/Taxable
C - Non-Taxable

PAGE NO. 31

PROD. NO. ______ PROD. TITLE ______ DATE: ______

4100 SECOND UNIT—SUMMARY

ACCT NO.	DESCRIPTION	PAGE NO.	BUDGET	TOTALS
01	Director (See Acct 1220)	32A		
02	Choreographer	32A		
03	Dialogue Director	32A		
04	Cast	32A		
19	Fringe Benefits & Payroll Taxes	32A		
	TOTAL SECOND UNIT ABOVE THE LINE			
20	Production Department	32A		
21	Extra Talent	32B		
22	Art Department	32B		
23	Set Construction	32B		
24	Set Dressing	32B		
25	Prop Department	32B		
26	Picture Vehicles	32B		
27	Special Effects	32B		
28	Camera Department	32B		
31	Sound Department	32C		
32	Grip Department	32C		
33	Lighting Department	32C		
34	Wardrobe	32C		
35	Makeup & Hair Dressing	32C		
36	Set Operations	32C		
40	Location Expenses	32D		

SUBTOTAL THIS PAGE ______

(CONTINUED ON NEXT PAGE)

PAGE NO. 32

PROD. NO. ____________ PROD. TITLE ____________ DATE: ____________

4100 SECOND UNIT—SUMMARY (Cont'd)

ACCT NO.	DESCRIPTION	PAGE NO.	BUDGET	TOTALS
45	Animals	32D		
46	Transportation	32E		
47	Film/Sound & Lab	32E		
48	Expenses (Rentals & Purchases)	32F		
49	Fringe Benefits & Payroll Taxes	32G		
85	Additional Expenses	32G		
95	Miscellaneous	32G		
99	Loss, Damage & Repair	32G		

SUBTOTALS THIS PAGE	
SUBTOTALS FROM PREVIOUS PAGE	
TOTAL SECOND UNIT BELOW THE LINE	
TOTAL SECOND UNIT ABOVE THE LINE	

TOTAL ACCOUNT 4100 ____________

PAGE NO. 32A

PROD. NO. ______ PROD. TITLE ______ DATE: ______

4100 SECOND UNIT

NO.	TITLE	DAYS					SUBTOTALS		
		PREP	SHOOT	WRAP	TOTAL	RATE	A	B	C
01	Director								
02	Choreographer								
03	Dialogue Director								
							TOTAL		

04	CAST NAME & STUNTS	DAYS					SUBTOTALS		
		PREP	SHOOT	WRAP	TOTAL	RATE	A	B	C
	Welfare Worker/Teacher								
							TOTAL		

19	FRINGE BENEFITS & PAYROLL TAXES/ABOVE-THE-LINE SECOND UNIT	AMOUNT	TOTALS
	Payroll Taxes & Comp. Ins.		
	Pension		
	Health & Welfare		

TOTAL SECOND UNIT ABOVE THE LINE	

20	PRODUCTION DEPARTMENT	DAYS					SUBTOTALS		
		PREP	SHOOT	WRAP	TOTAL	RATE	A	B	C
	Production Mgr.								
	1st Asst. Director								
	2nd Asst. Director								
	Location Mgr.								
	Production Acct.								
	D.G.A. Trainee								
	P.A.'s								
	Script Supervisor								
	Prod. Office Coord.								
	Additional Clerical								
	Technical Advisor								
							TOTAL		

TOTAL	

PAGE NO. 32B

PROD. NO. ______ PROD. TITLE ______ DATE: ______

4100	SECOND UNIT — (Cont'd)											
21	EXTRA TALENT									SUBTOTALS		
	DAY NO.	NO.	RATE	DAY NO.	NO.	RATE	DAY NO.	NO.	RATE	A	B	C
	1			4			7					
	2			5			8					
	3			6			9					
										TOTAL		

22	ART DEPARTMENT	DAYS					SUBTOTALS		
		PREP	SHOOT	WRAP	TOTAL	RATE	A	B	C
	Prod. Designer								
	Art Director								
							TOTAL		

23	SET CONSTRUCTION	DAYS					SUBTOTALS		
		PREP	SHOOT	WRAP	TOTAL	RATE	A	B	C
	Const. Coordinator								
	Const. Labor								
							TOTAL		

24	SET DRESSING	DAYS					SUBTOTALS		
		PREP	SHOOT	WRAP	TOTAL	RATE	A	B	C
	Set Decorator								
	Swing Gang-Leadman								
							TOTAL		

25	PROP DEPARTMENT	DAYS					SUBTOTALS		
		PREP	SHOOT	WRAP	TOTAL	RATE	A	B	C
	Prop Master								
	Asst. Propmaster								
							TOTAL		

26	PICTURE VEHICLES	DAYS					SUBTOTALS		
		PREP	SHOOT	WRAP	TOTAL	RATE	A	B	C
	Vehicle #1 Driver / Owner								
	Vehicle #2 Driver / Owner								
	Vehicle #3 Driver / Owner								
							TOTAL		

27	SPECIAL EFFECTS DEPT.	DAYS					SUBTOTALS		
		PREP	SHOOT	WRAP	TOTAL	RATE	A	B	C
	Special Effects Man								
							TOTAL		

28	CAMERA DEPARTMENT	DAYS					SUBTOTALS		
		PREP	SHOOT	WRAP	TOTAL	RATE	A	B	C
	Director of Photography								
	Camera Operator								
	1st A. C.								
	2nd A. C.								
							TOTAL		

PAGE NO. 32C

PROD. NO. ______ PROD. TITLE ______ DATE: ______

4100 SECOND UNIT—(Cont'd)

31	SOUND DEPARTMENT	DAYS					SUBTOTALS		
		PREP	SHOOT	WRAP	TOTAL	RATE	A	B	C
	Mixer								
	Boom Operator								
							TOTAL		

32	GRIP DEPARTMENT	DAYS					SUBTOTALS		
		PREP	SHOOT	WRAP	TOTAL	RATE	A	B	C
	Key Grip								
	2nd Company Grip								
	Company Grip								
							TOTAL		

33	LIGHTING DEPARTMENT	DAYS					SUBTOTALS		
		PREP	SHOOT	WRAP	TOTAL	RATE	A	B	C
	Gaffer								
	Best Boy								
	Electrician								
							TOTAL		

34	WARDROBE DEPARTMENT	DAYS					SUBTOTALS		
		PREP	SHOOT	WRAP	TOTAL	RATE	A	B	C
	Designer								
	Wardrobe Woman								
	Wardrobe Man								
							TOTAL		

35	MAKE-UP AND HAIRDRESSING	DAYS					SUBTOTALS		
		PREP	SHOOT	WRAP	TOTAL	RATE	A	B	C
	Make-up Artist								
	Hair Stylist								
							TOTAL		

36	SET OPERATIONS	DAYS					SUBTOTALS		
		PREP	SHOOT	WRAP	TOTAL	RATE	A	B	C
	Craft Serviceman								
	Policeman								
	Fireman								
	Watchman								
	First Aid/Nurse								
	Doctor								
							TOTAL		

PAGE NO. 32D

PROD. NO. ______ PROD. TITLE ______ DATE: ______

4100	SECOND UNIT—(Cont'd)								
40	LOCATION EXPENSE	DAYS					SUBTOTALS		
		PREP	SHOOT	WRAP	TOTAL	RATE	A	B	C
	Location Contact								
	Interpreters								
	Location Site Rental								
							TOTAL		

45	ANIMALS	DAYS					SUBTOTALS		
		PREP	SHOOT	WRAP	TOTAL	RATE	A	B	C
	Animals								
	Wrangler/Trainer								
							TOTAL		

46A	TRANSPORTATION (LABOR)	DAYS					SUBTOTALS		
		PREP	SHOOT	WRAP	TOTAL	RATE	A	B	C
	Driver 1								
	Driver 2								
	Driver 3								
	Driver 4								
	Driver 5								
	Driver 6								
	Driver 7								
	Driver 8								
							TOTAL		

LOCATION EXPENSE—DETAIL

PAGE NO. 32E

PROD. NO. ____________ PROD. TITLE ____________ DATE: ____________

46 TRANSPORTATION, LODGING, MEALS—SECOND UNIT

POSITION/NAME	DESTINATION (RT)	AIRFARES			LODGING (PER DIEM)			MEALS (PER DIEM)				
		NO. FLIGHTS	RATE	SUBTOTAL	NO. DAYS	RATE	SUBTOTAL	NO. DAYS		RATE	SUBTOTAL	TOTALS
									B			
									L			
									D			
									B			
									L			
									D			
									B			
									L			
									D			
									B			
									L			
									D			
									B			
									L			
									D			
									B			
									L			
									D			
									B			
									L			
									D			
									B			
									L			
									D			
									B			
									L			
									D			
									B			
									L			
									D			
			SUBTOTALS									
									TOTAL DETAIL ACCT 46			

SAMPLE

A - Fringeable/Taxable
B - Non-Fringeable/Taxable
C - Non-Taxable

PAGE NO. 32F

PROD. NO. ________ PROD. TITLE ________ DATE: ________

4100 SECOND UNIT—(Cont'd)

48A EQUIPMENT AND MATERIALS/RENTALS

DEPARTMENT	DESCRIPTION	SUBTOTAL
	TOTAL	

48B EQUIPMENT AND MATERIALS/PURCHASES

DEPARTMENT	DESCRIPTION	SUBTOTAL
	TOTAL	

PAGE NO. 32G

PROD. NO. ____________ PROD. TITLE ____________ DATE: ____________

4100	SECOND UNIT—(Cont'd)				
49	FRINGE BENEFITS AND PAYROLL TAXES (2ND UNIT)				
	DESCRIPTION	PAYROLL	PENSION	HEALTH & WELFARE	TOTALS
	DGA $ ____	%	%	%	
	PGA $ ____	%	%	%	
	WGA $ ____	%	%	%	
	SAG $ ____	%	%	%	
	IATSE $ ____	%	%	%	
	NABET $ ____	%	%	%	
	OTHER OR ALLOW $ ____	%	%	%	
	SUBTOTALS				

85	ADDITIONAL EXPENSES	
	TOTAL	
95	MISCELLANEOUS	
	TOTAL	
99	LOSS, DAMAGE, REPAIR	
	TOTAL	

TOTAL SECOND UNIT BELOW-THE-LINE	
TOTAL SECOND UNIT ABOVE-THE-LINE	

TOTAL ACCT 4100	

PAGE NO. 33

PROD. NO. ______ PROD. TITLE ______ DATE: ______

4200	TESTS (USE SECOND UNIT FOR DETAILED TEST BUDGET — ACCT 4100)	SUBTOTALS		
ACCT. NO.	DESCRIPTION	A	B	C
47	Film/Sound Lab			
	Negative Film			
	Sound Negative			
	Film Negative Develop			
	Film One Light Print			
	Color Corrected Dailies			
	Sound Transfers—Stock			
	Sound Transfers—Labor			
85	Additional Expenses			
95	Miscellaneous			
99	Loss, Damage, Repair			
	SUBTOTALS			
	TOTAL ACCT 4200			

SAMPLE

A - Fringeable/Taxable C - Non-Taxable
B - Non-Fringeable/Taxable

PAGE NO. 34

PROD. NO. ______________ PROD. TITLE ______________ DATE: ______________

4300 MINIATURE DEPARTMENT

ACCT. NO.	DESCRIPTION		LOCAL / ON LOC.	DAYS / WEEKS PREP	SHOOT	WRAP	TOTAL	RATE	SUBTOTALS A	B	C
01	Supervisor		Local								
			On Loc.								
			Local								
	Labor	No.	On Loc.								
05	Painters		Local								
			On Loc.								
			Local								
			On Loc.								
06	Scenic Artists		Local								
			On Loc.								
			Local								
			On Loc.								
07	Carpenters		Local								
			On Loc.								
			Local								
			On Loc.								
08	Propmakers		Local								
			On Loc.								
			Local								
			On Loc.								
			Local								
			On Loc.								
			Local								
			On Loc.								
	Additional Hire		Local								
			On Loc.								
15	Labor (See Detail Page 34A)										
20	Materials (See Detail Page 34A)										
22	Rigging (See Detail Page 34A)										
24	Striking (See Detail Page 34A)										
30	Rentals (See Detail Page 34B)										
40	Purchases (See Detail Page 34B)										
85	Additional Expense										
95	Miscellaneous										
99	Loss, Damage, Repair										
								SUBTOTALS			
								TOTAL ACCT 4300			

A - Fringeable/Taxable
B - Non-Fringeable/Taxable
C - Non-Taxable

PAGE NO. 34A

PROD. NO. ____________ PROD. TITLE ____________ DATE: ____________

4315, 4320, 4322, 4324 MINIATURES—DETAIL

SET NO.	SCENE NAME / NO. DESCRIPTION	(4315) LABOR	(4320) MATERIALS	(4322) RIGGING	(4324) STRIKING	SUBTOTALS A	SUBTOTALS B	SUBTOTALS C
	SUBTOTALS							
	TOTAL DETAIL ACCT 4315, 4320, 4322, 4324							

A - Fringeable/Taxable
B - Non-Fringeable/Taxable
C - Non-Taxable

PAGE NO. 34B

PROD. NO. ______ PROD. TITLE ______ DATE: ______

ACCTS 4330 & 4340 MINIATURES—DETAIL								
SET	SCENE NAME/NO.	ITEM		RENTALS			PURCHASES	✓
NO.	DESCRIPTION	QTY	DESCRIPTION	TIME	RATE	AMOUNT	AMOUNT	
SUBTOTALS								
TOTAL DETAIL ACCTS 4330 & 4340								

A - Fringeable/Taxable C - Non-Taxable
B - Non-Fringeable/Taxable ✓ - Recoupable

PAGE NO. 35

PROD. NO. ______ PROD. TITLE ______ DATE: ______

4400 PROCESS DEPARTMENT

ACCT. NO.	DESCRIPTION	LOCAL/ ON LOC.	DAYS/WEEKS PREP	SHOOT	WRAP	TOTAL	RATE	SUBTOTALS A	B	C
01	Projectionist	Local								
		On Loc.								
		Local								
		On Loc.								
02	Camera Man	Local								
		On Loc.								
		Local								
		On Loc.								
03	Camera Operator	Local								
		On Loc.								
		Local								
		On Loc.								
04	Asst. Camera Man	Local								
		On Loc.								
		Local								
		On Loc.								
05	Electrical	Local								
		On Loc.								
06	Grip	Local								
		On Loc.								
07	Matte Artist	Local								
		On Loc.								
08	Matte Crew	Local								
		On Loc.								
		Local								
		On Loc.								
09	Rear Screen									
10	Front Screen									
12	Mock Up									
30	Rentals									
40	Purchases									
85	Additional Expense									
95	Miscellaneous									
99	Loss, Damage, Repair									
							SUBTOTALS			
							TOTAL ACCT 4400			

SAMPLE

A - Fringeable/Taxable
B - Non-Fringeable/Taxable
C - Non-Taxable

PAGE NO. 36

PROD. NO. ______________ PROD. TITLE ______________ DATE: ______________

4500 ANIMALS

ACCT. NO.	DESCRIPTION	LOCAL/ ON LOC.	DAYS/WEEKS PREP	SHOOT	WRAP	TOTAL	RATE	SUBTOTALS A	B	C
01	Head Wrangler	Local								
		On Loc.								
02	Additional Wrangler	Local								
		On Loc.								
03	Trainers	Local								
		On Loc.								
		Local								
		On Loc.								
04	Handlers	Local								
		On Loc.								
		Local								
		On Loc.								
		Local								
		On Loc.								
		Local								
		On Loc.								
		Local								
		On Loc.								
		Local								
		On Loc.								
		Local								
		On Loc.								
		Local								
		On Loc.								
	Additional Hire	Local								
		On Loc.								
30	Rentals (See Detail Page 36A)									
40	Purchases (See Detail Page 36A)									
50	Animal Maintenance									
60	Special Transportation									
75	Travel and Living (List on Acct 4005)									
85	Additional Expense									
95	Miscellaneous									
99	Loss, Damage, Repair									
							SUBTOTALS			
							TOTAL ACCT 4500			

A - Fringeable/Taxable
B - Non-Fringeable/Taxable
C - Non-Taxable

PAGE NO. 36A

PROD. NO. ____________ PROD. TITLE ____________ DATE: ____________

ACCTS 4530 & 4540 ANIMALS—DETAIL

SET	SCENE NAME/NO.	ANIMALS			RENTALS		PURCHASES	✓
NO.	DESCRIPTION	QTY	DESCRIPTION	W/H/T	RATE	AMOUNT	AMOUNT	
				SUBTOTALS				
			TOTAL DETAIL ACCTS NO. 4530 & 4540					

A - Fringeable/Taxable
B - Non-Fringeable/Taxable
C - Non-Taxable

✓ = Recoupable
W/H/T = Wrangler, Handler or Trainer

PAGE NO. 37

PROD. NO. ______ PROD. TITLE ______ DATE: ______

4600	TRANSPORTATION DEPARTMENT	SUBTOTALS		
ACCT. NO.	DESCRIPTION	A	B	C
01	Coordinator			
02	Drivers—Captain and Co-Captain (See Detail Pages 37 A & B)			
03	Drivers (See Detail Pages 37 A & B)			
30	Vehicles—Rentals/Local (See Detail Pages 37 A & B)			
35	Vehicles—Rentals/Location (See Detail Pages 37 A & B)			
50	Gas and Oil			
55	Gas and Oil — Generator			
57	Messenger Service			
59	Deliveries and Pick-Ups			
60	Pick-Up — Dailies (Also See Location Acct 4000)			
61	Taxis and Limos			
63	Car Allowances (See Detail Page 37D)			
65	Vehicle Mileage (See Detail Page 37B)			
67	Mileage Allowances — Crew and Cast (See Detail Page 37E)			
69	Permits, Tolls, Parking and Fees (See Detail Page 37B)			
70	Maintenance (See Detail Page 37B)			
71	Storage			
73	Trucks to Distant Location—Expenses			
75	Truck Rigging/Shelving			
85	Additional Expenses			
95	Miscellaneous			
99	Loss, Damage, Repair			
	SUBTOTALS			
	TOTAL ACCT 4600			

A - Fringeable/Taxable
B - Non-Fringeable/Taxable
C - Non-Taxable

TRANSPORTATION—DETAIL

PAGE NO. 37A

NOTE: For varying times and rates indicate PREP/SHOOT/WRAP

DESCRIPTION	DRIVERS LOCAL		DRIVERS LOCATION		TOTAL	EQUIPMENT LOCAL		EQUIPMENT LOCATION		TOTAL
	WEEKS	RATE	WEEKS	RATE		WEEKS	RATE	WEEKS	RATE	
Coordinator										
				4601 Total						
Captain										
Co-Captain										
Dispatcher										
				4602 Total						
Mechanic										
Production Van (Grip/Electric)										
Camera/Sound Truck										
Prop Truck										
Special Effects Truck										
Wardrobe Truck										
Wardrobe Trailer										
Makeup/Hair Truck										
Makeup/Hair Trailer										
Set Dressing Truck										
Set Dressing Wagon										
Construction Truck										
Construction Crew Cab										
Honeywagons										
Motor Homes										
Station Wagons										
Crew Bus										
Extra Bus										
Mini Vans/Crew Cab										
People Mover										
Catering Truck (Fee)										
				4603 Total		4630 Sub.		4635 Sub.		
			CONTINUED ON NEXT PAGE					CONTINUED ON NEXT PAGE		

SAMPLE

TRANSPORTATION—DETAIL (Cont'd)

PAGE NO. 37B

NOTE: For varying times and rates indicate PREP/SHOOT/WRAP

DESCRIPTION	DRIVERS					EQUIPMENT				
	LOCAL		LOCATION		TOTAL	LOCAL		LOCATION		TOTAL
	WEEKS	RATE	WEEKS	RATE		WEEKS	RATE	WEEKS	RATE	
Limo										
Camera Car/Insert Car										
Car Carrier										
Water Wagon										
Pick-up Trucks										
Crane Driver										
Fuel Truck										
Ambulance (See Location Acct 4000)										
Fork Lift										
Tow Trucks										
Generator										
Other Production Cars										
Additional Hire										
	Subtotal From Previous Page									
	TOTAL DETAIL 4603					Total Det. 4630		Total Det. 4635		
65 Vehicle Mileage										
69 Permits, Tolls, Parking and Fees										
70 Maintenance										
71 Storage										

TRANSPORTATION—DETAIL

PAGE NO. 37C

NOTE: For varying times and rates indicate PREP/SHOOT/WRAP

DESCRIPTION	DRIVERS					EQUIPMENT				
	LOCAL		LOCATION		TOTAL	LOCAL		LOCATION		TOTAL
	WEEKS	RATE	WEEKS	RATE		WEEKS	RATE	WEEKS	RATE	

PAGE NO. 37D

PROD. NO. ______________ PROD. TITLE ______________ DATE: ______________

4663 CAR ALLOWANCES—DETAIL

DEPARTMENT	POSTION / NAME	WEEKS / DAYS	RATE	TOTAL
TOTAL DETAIL ACCT 3400				

A - Fringeable/Taxable
B - Non-Fringeable/Taxable
C - Non-Taxable

PAGE NO. 37E

PROD. NO. ____________ PROD. TITLE ____________ DATE: ____________

4667 MILEAGE—DETAIL

DAY NO.	NO. PEOPLE	SET NO. / LOCATION	MILES	RATE	TOTAL
TOTAL DETAIL ACCT 4667					

A - Fringeable/Taxable
B - Non-Fringeable/Taxable
C - Non-Taxable

PAGE NO. 38

PROD. NO. ____________ PROD. TITLE ____________ DATE: ____________

4700	PRODUCTION RAWSTOCK AND LABORATORY				SUBTOTALS		
ACCT. NO.	DESCRIPTION	FOOTAGE	RATE	AMOUNT	A	B	C
01	Picture Negative Rawstock						
	1/4" Audio Tape Rawstock						
10	Picture Negative Developing						
	Forced Developing						
20	Picture Negative Print						
	One Lite Print						
	Color Corrected Dailies						
35	Sound Transfer						
	Stock						
	Labor						
45	Video						
	Video Tape Rawstock						
	Film to Tape Transfer						
	3/4" Tape Time Code Copies						
50	Special Lab Work						
85	Additional Expenses						
90	Sales Tax on Acct 4700						
95	Miscellaneous						
	Reels, Cases, Boxes, Etc.						
	Picture Leader						
99	Loss, Damage, Repair						
	SUBTOTALS						
	TOTAL ACCT 4700						

A - Fringeable/Taxable C - Non-Taxable
B - Non-Fringeable/Taxable

PAGE NO. 39

PROD. NO. ______ PROD. TITLE ______ DATE: ______

4900 FRINGE BENEFITS AND PAYROLL TAXES—BELOW-THE-LINE					
ACCT NO.	DESCRIPTION	PAYROLL	PENSION	HEALTH & WELFARE	TOTALS
01	DGA $ ______	% ______	% ______	% ______	
02	PGA $ ______	% ______	% ______	% ______	
03	WGA $ ______	% ______	% ______	% ______	
04	SAG $ ______	% ______	% ______	% ______	
05	IATSE $ ______	% ______	% ______	% ______	
06	NABET $ ______	% ______	% ______	% ______	
07	OTHER $ ______	% ______	% ______	% ______	
10	or Allow				

SUBTOTALS				

TOTAL ACCT 4900 ______

TOTAL COST BELOW-THE-LINE ______

A - Fringeable/Taxable
B - Non-Fringeable/Taxable
C - Non-Taxable

PAGE NO. 40

PROD. NO. ______ PROD. TITLE ______ DATE: ______

5000 FILM EDITING DEPARTMENT

ACCT. NO.	DESCRIPTION	LOCAL/ ON LOC.	DAYS/WEEKS PREP	SHOOT	WRAP	TOTAL	RATE	SUBTOTALS A	B	C
01	Post Production Supervisor	Local								
		On Loc.								
		Local								
		On Loc.								
02	Editor	Local								
		On Loc.								
		Local								
		On Loc.								
03	Asst. Editors	Local								
		On Loc.								
		Local								
		On Loc.								
04	Apprentice Editor	Local								
		On Loc.								
		Local								
		On Loc.								
05	Looping Editors	Local								
		On Loc.								
06	Asst. Looping Editor	Local								
		On Loc.								
		Local								
		On Loc.								
08	Music Editor	Local								
		On Loc.								
09	Asst. Music Editor	Local								
		On Loc.								
	SUBTOTALS THIS PAGE									
	CONTINUED ON NEXT PAGE									

A - Fringeable/Taxable
B - Non-Fringeable/Taxable
C - Non-Taxable

PAGE NO. 41

PROD. NO. ______ PROD. TITLE ______ DATE: ______

5000 FILM EDITING DEPARTMENT—(Cont'd)

ACCT. NO.	DESCRIPTION	LOCAL / ON LOC.	DAYS / WEEKS PREP	SHOOT	WRAP	TOTAL	RATE	SUBTOTALS A	B	C
07	Sound Effects Editor & Asst.	Local								
		On Loc.								
		Local								
		On Loc.								
08	Projection Labor	Local								
		On Loc.								
		Local								
		On Loc.								
09	Dialogue Transcription	Local								
		On Loc.								
11	Off Line Editing - Labor	Local								
		On Loc.								
12	Cutting Continuity	Local								
		On Loc.								
13	Secretary	Local								
		On Loc.								
14	Librarian	Local								
		On Loc.								
		Local								
		On Loc.								
15	Coding Maintenance	Local								
		On Loc.								
		Local								
		On Loc.								
16	Shipping & Messengers	Local								
		On Loc.								
30	Rentals									
	Cutting Room									
	Editing Equipment									
	Projection Room									
	Music & Effects									
	Off-Line Editing									
40	Purchases									
	Supplies									
	Video Transfers									
80	Preview Expenses									
85	Additional Expenses									
95	Miscellaneous									
99	Loss, Damage, Repair									
	SUBTOTALS FROM PREVIOUS PAGE									
	SUBTOTALS THIS PAGE									
	TOTAL ACCT 5000									

A - Fringeable/Taxable
B - Non-Fringeable/Taxable
C - Non-Taxable

PAGE NO. 42

PROD. NO. ______ PROD. TITLE ______ DATE: ______

5100 MUSIC					SUBTOTALS		
ACCT. NO.	DESCRIPTION	TIME	RATE	AMT.	A	B	C
01	Composer						
02	Lyricist						
03	Music Coordinator						
04	Arrangers and Orchestrators						
05	Director/Conductor						
06	Copyists and Proof Readers						
07	Musicians						
08	Singers						
09	Rehearsal Pianist						
10	Coaches—Instrumental/Vocal						
11	Labor on Music Stage						
12	Labor Moving Instruments						
13	Cartage						
14	Sync Rights/Music License Fees						
15	Original Songs Purchased						
30	Rentals						
	Instruments						
	Studio—Rehearsal						
	Studio—Recording						
40	Purchases						
85	Additional Expenses						
95	Miscellaneous						
99	Loss, Damage, Repair						
	SUBTOTALS						
	TOTAL ACCT 5100						

A - Fringeable/Taxable
B - Non-Fringeable/Taxable
C - Non-Taxable

PAGE NO. 43

PROD. NO. ____________ PROD. TITLE ____________ DATE: ____________

5200	FILM EFFECTS				SUBTOTALS		
ACCT. NO.	DESCRIPTION	QTY.	RATE	AMT.	A	B	C
01	Consultants						
02	Opticals						
	Fades, Dissolves, etc.						
	Special Opticals-Montages,						
	Split Screen, Computer Graphics, etc.						
	Backgrounds For Process						
03	Matte Shots (Also See Process Acct 4400)						
04	Inserts						
05	Animation						
06	Process Plates						
30	Rentals						
	Equipment						
40	Purchases						
	Film and Lab Charges						
	Materials and Supplies						
	Film-Picture Negative						
	Film-Interpositive						
	Film-Positive Print Negative						
85	Additional Expenses						
90	Sales Tax						
95	Miscellaneous						
99	Loss, Damage, Repair						
	SUBTOTALS						
	TOTAL ACCT 5200						

A - Fringeable/Taxable C - Non-Taxable
B - Non-Fringeable/Taxable

PAGE NO. 44

PROD. NO. ______ PROD. TITLE ______ DATE: ______

5300	TITLES DEPARTMENT				SUBTOTALS		
ACCT. NO.	DESCRIPTION	QTY.	RATE	AMT.	A	B	C
01	Title Design						
	Art, Lettering						
02	Title Filming						
03	Sub Titles						
30	Rentals						
	Equipment						
40	Purchases						
	Film and Lab Charges						
85	Additional Expenses						
90	Sales Tax						
95	Miscellaneous						
99	Loss, Damage, Repair						
				SUBTOTALS			
				TOTAL ACCT 5300			

A - Fringeable/Taxable
B - Non-Fringeable/Taxable
C - Non-Taxable

PAGE NO. 45

PROD. NO. ______ PROD. TITLE ______ DATE: ______

5400	POST-PRODUCTION SOUND				SUBTOTALS		
ACCT. NO.	DESCRIPTION	TIME	RATE	AMT.	A	B	C
01	Sound Transfers — Labor/Facilities						
	Daily Reprints						
	Narration/Loops						
	Sound Effects						
	Music						
	Mix						
02	Magnetic Film						
	Narration/Loop Recording Masters						
	Narration/Loop Transfers						
	Sound Effects Recording Masters						
	Sound Effects Transfers						
	Music Recording Masters						
	Music Dub-Down Masters						
	Music Transfers						
	Dupe Work Track Transfers						
	Dubbing Masters						
	Dub Transfers						
	Music File Copy						
03	Sound Effects Recording ADR						
04	Dolby						
05	Foley						
06	Dialogue Replacement						
	Looping/Narration						
07	Vocals						
08	Music Recording						
09	Dub Downs						
10	Re-Recording (Pre-Dubbing)						
	Preview						
11	Miscellaneous Labor						
	Set Up Scoring Dubbing						
12	Sound Negative Raw Stock						
	35mm						
13	Foreign Delivery Requirements						
	Music Tracks						
14	Playback Preparation — Labor						
15	Daily Transfers — Material						
16	Reprint Transfers						
17	Playback Preparation — Material						
30	Rentals						
	Facilities (Post Production)						
40	Purchases						
85	Additional Expenses						
95	Miscellaneous						
99	Loss, Damage, Repair						
				SUBTOTALS			
				TOTAL ACCT 5400			

A - Fringeable/Taxable
B - Non-Fringeable/Taxable
C - Non-Taxable

PAGE NO. 46

PROD. NO. ______ PROD. TITLE ______ DATE: ______

5500	POST-PRODUCTION FILM AND LAB				SUBTOTALS		
ACCT. NO.	DESCRIPTION	QTY.	RATE	AMT.	A	B	C
01	Editorial Reprints — 1 Lite Color						
02	35mm Silent Timing Print						
03	35mm Composite Answer Print						
04	35mm Release Prints						
05	35mm Interpositive or C.R.I. (Prot. Master)						
06	35mm Internegatives						
07	1st Trial Composite Answer Print						
08	16mm Release Prints						
09	16mm Protective Master						
10	Reversal Prints Black & White						
11	35mm Sound Negative Dev. & Print						
12	16mm Sound Negative Dev. & Print						
13	Stock Footage—License Fees						
14	Stock Footage—Processing						
15	Negative Cutting						
16	Outside Lab Charges						
17	Transfer to Cassette						
18	Shipping Charges						
19	Network Requirements						
30	Rentals						
	Vault Rental						
40	Purchases						
	Picture Leader (Positive & Negative)						
	Reels						
	Cans						
	Video Cassettes						
	Videotape Dupes						
	Film Charges						
	Laboratory Charges						
85	Additional Expenses						
95	Miscellaneous						
99	Loss, Damage, Repair						
	SUBTOTALS						
	TOTAL ACCT 5500						

A - Fringeable/Taxable
B - Non-Fringeable/Taxable
C - Non-Taxable

PAGE NO. 47

PROD. NO. ______ PROD. TITLE ______ DATE: ______

5900	FRINGE BENEFITS AND PAYROLL TAXES—POST PRODUCTION				
ACCT NO.	DESCRIPTION	PAYROLL	PENSION	HEALTH & WELFARE	TOTALS
01	DGA $ ______	% ______	% ______	% ______	
02	PGA $ ______	% ______	% ______	% ______	
03	WGA $ ______	% ______	% ______	% ______	
04	SAG $ ______	% ______	% ______	% ______	
05	IATSE $ ______	% ______	% ______	% ______	
06	NABET $ ______	% ______	% ______	% ______	
10	OTHER $ ______	% ______	% ______	% ______	
	or Allow				

SUBTOTALS				

TOTAL ACCT 5900 ______

TOTAL COSTS—POST PRODUCTION ______

A - Fringeable/Taxable
B - Non-Fringeable/Taxable
C - Non-Taxable

PAGE NO. 48

PROD. NO. ____________ PROD. TITLE ____________ DATE: ____________

6000 PUBLICITY

ACCT. NO.	DESCRIPTION	LOCAL / ON LOC.	DAYS / WEEKS PREP	SHOOT	WRAP	TOTAL	RATE	SUBTOTALS A	B	C
01	Publicity Firm Fee	Local								
		On Loc.								
		Local								
		On Loc.								
02	Unit Publicist	Local								
		On Loc.								
		Local								
		On Loc.								
03	Still Photographer	Local								
		On Loc.								
		Local								
		On Loc.								
04	Special Photographer	Local								
		On Loc.								
		Local								
		On Loc.								
	Additional Hire	Local								
		On Loc.								
		Local								
		On Loc.								
05	Trailers	Local								
		On Loc.								
10	Consulting Fees	Local								
		On Loc.								
		Local								
		On Loc.								
30	Rentals									
	Camera Equipment									
30	Purchases									
	Film									
	Processing									
	Prints									
	Lab Expense									
85	Additional Expenses									
	Entertainment									
95	Miscellaneous									
99	Loss, Damage, Repair									
	SUBTOTALS									
	TOTAL ACCT 6000									

A - Fringeable/Taxable
B - Non-Fringeable/Taxable
C - Non-Taxable

PAGE NO. 49

PROD. NO. ____________ PROD. TITLE ____________ DATE: ____________

6100	INSURANCE		SUBTOTALS		
ACCT. NO.	DESCRIPTION	AMOUNT	A	B	C
01	Cast Insurance				
02	Negative Film Insurance				
03	Workman's Compensation Insurance				
04	Errors and Omission Insurance				
05	Faulty Raw Stock, Camera and Processing				
06	Comprehensive Liability Insurance				
07	Set, Props, and Wardrobe Insurance				
08	Extra Expense Insurance				
09	Miscellaneous Equipment Insurance				
10	Other Insurance				
	Local Insurance Requirement				
11	Medical Exams				
25	Extra Riders/Additional Insurance				
85	Additional Expenses				
95	Miscellaneous				
99	Loss, Damage, Repair				
		SUBTOTALS			
		TOTAL ACCT 6100			

A - Fringeable/Taxable
B - Non-Fringeable/Taxable
C - Non-Taxable

PAGE NO. 50

PROD. NO. ______ PROD. TITLE ______ DATE: ______

6200	GENERAL EXPENSE		SUBTOTALS		
ACCT. NO.	DESCRIPTION	RATE	A	B	C
01	Secretary				
02	Messenger Service				
03	Janitor/Cleaning Service				
04	Shipping (Also See Acct 3010)				
05	Courtesy Payments (Also See Accts 4029 & 3717)				
06	Accounting Service				
07	Production Services				
08	Entertainment				
	Meals (Also See Acct 4009)				
	Wrap Party				
09	Bank and Foreign Currency Exchange Cost				
10	Facility Sales Tax				
30	Rentals				
	Telephone & Telegraph (Also See Acct 4016)				
	Installation Charges (Also See Acct 4016)				
	Office (Also See Acct 4013)				
	Office Equip. (Also See Acct 4014)				
	Office Furniture (Also See Acct 4014)				
	Duplicating Machine (Also See Acct 4014)				
	Parking (Also See Acct 4095)				
	Data Processing				
	Storage				
40	Purchases				
	Office Supplies (Also See Acct 4012)				
	Stationery				
	Postage (Also See Acct 4011)				
	City License				
	MPAA Code Seal Fee				
85	Additional Expenses				
	Legal Fees				
	Legal Research				
	Accounting Fees				
	Preview Expenses				
90	Sales Tax				
95	Miscellaneous				
99	Loss, Damage, Repair				
		SUBTOTALS			
		TOTAL ACCT 6200			

A - Fringeable/Taxable
B - Non-Fringeable/Taxable
C - Non-Taxable

PAGE NO. 51

PROD. NO. ______ PROD. TITLE ______ DATE: ______

6900 FRINGE BENEFITS AND PAYROLL TAXES—OTHER COSTS					
ACCT NO.	DESCRIPTION	PAYROLL	PENSION	HEALTH & WELFARE	TOTALS
01	DGA $ ______	% ______	% ______	% ______	
05	IATSE $ ______	% ______	% ______	% ______	
06	NABET $ ______	% ______	% ______	% ______	
	OTHER $ ______	% ______	% ______	% ______	
	or Allow				

SUBTOTALS				

TOTAL ACCT 6900 ______

TOTAL ABOVE THE LINE ______

TOTAL BELOW THE LINE ______

TOTAL POST PRODUCTION ______

TOTAL OTHER COSTS ______

TOTAL DIRECT COST ______

A - Fringeable/Taxable
B - Non-Fringeable/Taxable
C - Non-Taxable

PAGE NO. 52

PROD. NO. ________ PROD. TITLE ________ DATE: ________

7500	CONTINGENCY	
ACCT NO.	DESCRIPTION	TOTALS
01	10% x $________ (Total Direct Cost)	
	TOTAL ACCT 7500	

7600	COMPLETION BOND (OPTIONAL)	
01	6% x $________ (Total Direct Cost + Contingency)	
	TOTAL ACCT 7600	

7700	OVERHEAD	
01	________% x $________	
	TOTAL ACCT 7700	

7800	INTEREST, FINANCING CHARGES, FINDERS' FEES	
01	Interest	
02	Financing Charges	
03	Finders' Fees	
	TOTAL ACCT 7800	
	TOTAL NEGATIVE COST	

8000	DEFERMENTS			
01	DATE PAYABLE	TO WHOM	AMOUNT	
			TOTAL ACCT 8000	
TOTAL NEGATIVE COST (INCLUDING DEFERMENTS)				

A - Fringeable/Taxable
B - Non-Fringeable/Taxable
C - Non-Taxable

PRODUCTION FORMS

Production Forms

NOTE: The names, addresses, figures, etc., which are contained in the sample forms are for information and example purposes only. They are not to be construed as actual forms used during the making of *THE CONVERSATION.*

ACTORS
DAY OUT OF DAYS

NOV. 24, 19-- DATE

FRANCIS FORD COPPOLA PRODS. — PRODUCTION COMPANY

THE CONVERSATION — PRODUCTION TITLE/NUMBER

NOVEMBER 19-- — SCRIPT DATE

F.F. COPPOLA / F. ROOS / M. SKAGER — PRODUCER

FRANCIS F. COPPOLA — DIRECTOR

CLARK PAYLOW — PRODUCTION MANAGER./ASSISTANT DIRECTOR

Rehearsal-R Hold-H
Started-S Travel-T
Worked-W Finish-F
On Call-C

		Day Number	1	2	3	4	5	6			7	8	9	10	11			12	13	14	15	16			17	18	19	20	21		HOLIDAY BREAK
		Date	11/26	27	28	29	30	12/1	2	3	4	5	6	7	8	9	10	11	12	13	14	15	16	17	18	19	20	21	22	23	
		Day of the Week	S	M	T	W	T	F	S	S	M	T	W	T	F	S	S	M	T	W	T	F	S	S	M	T	W	T	F	S	
No.	Character	Last																													
1	HARRY CAUL	GENE HACKMAN	S/W	W	W	W	W	W						W				W	W	W	W	W									
2	ANN	CINDY WILLIAMS				S/W	W	W			W	W	W	W				V.O	W	W	V/O	V/O									
3	MARK	FREDERIC FORREST																													
4	MR. C.	ROBERT DUVALL																													
5	STANLEY	JOHN CAZALE																													
6	DAVE MEYERS																														
7	MARTIN	HARRISON FORD																													
8	WILLIAM P. MORAN																														
9	MEREDITH																														
10	MILLARD																														
11	MRS. GOETNER																														
12	RON KELLER																														
13	MRS. CORSITTO																														
14	BOB																														
15	BOB'S WIFE																														
16	AMY	TERI GARR																													
17	LURLEEN																														
18	MALE SEC'Y								SATURDAY	SUNDAY						SATURDAY	SUNDAY														
19	TONY																														
20	MALE RECEPT.																														
21	MIME																														
22	YOUNG MAN																														
23	YOUNG WOMAN																														
24	SHOPPER #1																														
25	SHOPPER #2																														
26	SHOPPER #3																														
27	LAUNDRY LADY																														
28	#27's LITTLE BOY																														
29	WOMAN #1 IN ELEV.																														
30	WOMAN #2 IN ELEV.																														

TAPE FIRST PAGE HERE

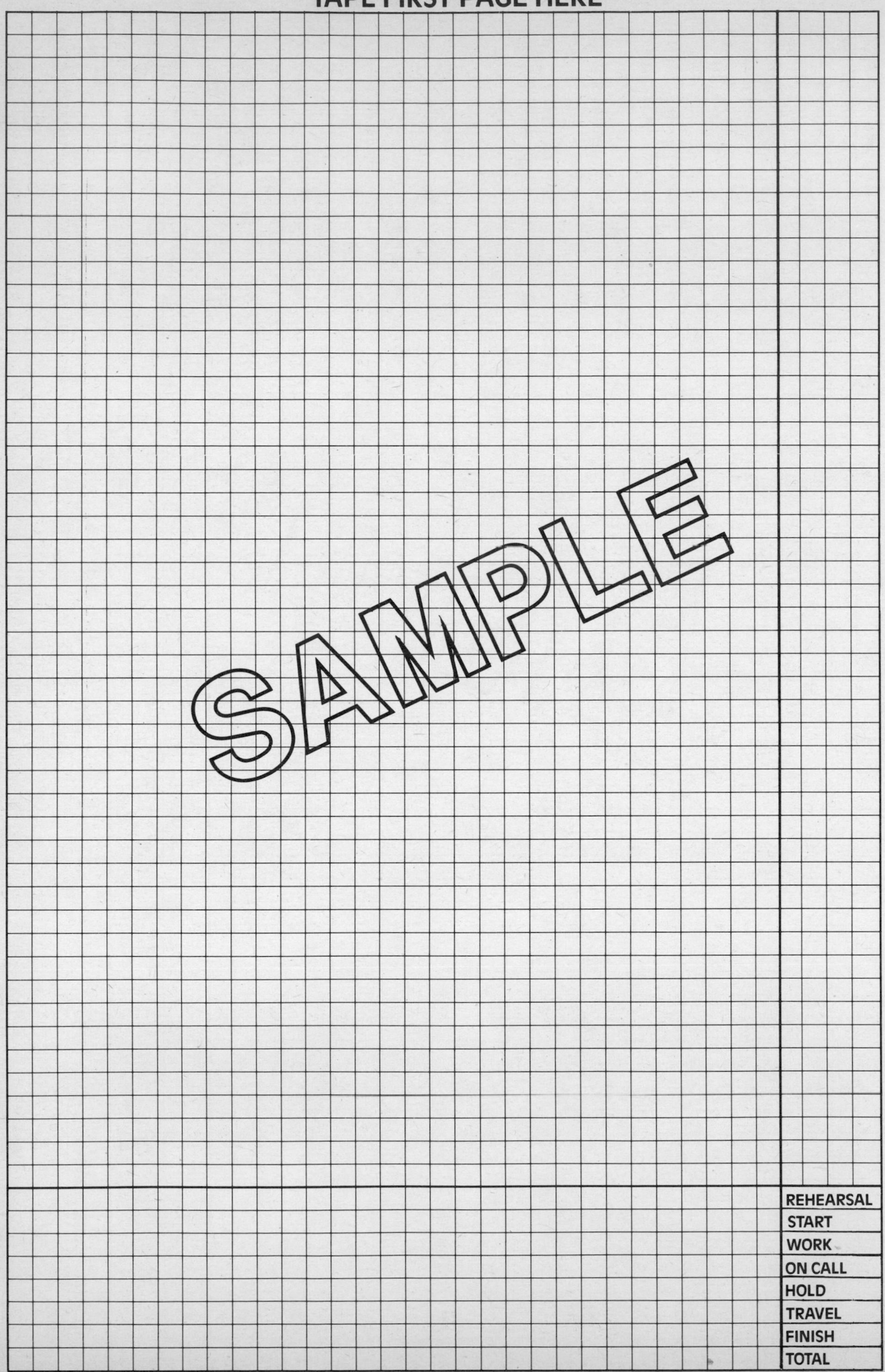

ACTOR'S DEAL MEMO

FRANCIS FORD COPPOLA PRODS.
PRODUCTION COMPANY

THE CONVERSATION
PRODUCTION TITLE / NO.

NOV. 24, 19--
DATE

H. FORD
ACTOR'S NAME

123 MAIN STREET
LOS ANGELES, CA 90000
ACTOR'S ADDRESS

213/555-5555
PHONE NO.

AMY AGENT
AGENT'S NAME

AMY AGENT, INC.
456 MAIN STREET
AGENT'S ADDRESS

213/999-9999
PHONE NO.

MARTIN
ACTOR'S PART

123-45-6789
S.S. NO./EMPLOYER I.D. NO.

DEAL: SCALE + 10%

X
DAILY

WEEKLY

GUARANTEE: 5 DAYS

SAMPLE

DETAIL: WORKS WEEK #3 AND WEEK #9
DROP-AND-PICK-UP

BILLING: AT PRODUCER'S DISCRETION

C. Payton
APPROVAL

CAST LIST

NOV. 24, 19--
DATE

PAGE ______ OF ______

FRANCIS FORD COPPOLA PRODS.
PRODUCTION COMPANY

THE CONVERSATION
PRODUCTION TITLE

PRODUCTION NO.

CHARACTER	NAME AND ADDRESS	TELEPHONE NO.
1. HARRY CAUL	GENE HACKMAN UNION SQUARE HOTEL UNION SQUARE SAN FRANCISCO, CA 94000	415-999-9999
2. ANN	CINDY WILLIAMS UNION SQUARE HOTEL UNION SQUARE SAN FRANCISCO, CA 94000	415-999-9999
3. MARK	FREDERIC FORREST UNION SQUARE HOTEL UNION SQUARE SAN FRANCISCO, CA 94000	415-999-9999
4. MR. "C"	ROBERT DUVALL 123 MAIN STREET BEVERLY HILLS, CA	213-999-9999
5. STANLEY	JOHN CAZALE 123 MAIN STREET NEW YORK CITY, NEW YORK 10000	212-999-9999
6. CONT'D.		

CAST / SCENE NUMBER BREAKDOWN

PAGE 1 OF ______

PRODUCTION TITLE: THE CONVERSATION NO. ______ DATE: NOV. 24, 19--

CAST MEMBER	SCENE NUMBER(S)
HARRY CAUL (GENE HACKMAN)	1-9, 12, 14, 15, 16, 27, 29, 34, 35, 36, 37, 38, 39, 40, 41, 42, 43, 44, 45, 46, 47, 48, 49, 50, 51, 52, 53, 54, 55, 56, 57, 58, 59, 60, 61, 63, 65, 67, 69, 70, 72, 73 74, 75, 76, 77, 78, 79, 80, 82, 83, 84, 85, 86, 88, 89, 90, 91, 92, 93, 94, 95, 96,
HARRY CONT'D.	97, 98, 99, 100, 101, 102, 104, 105, 106, 108-119, 121, 122, 124, 126-159, 161-181, 183, 184, 186-283, 287, 292, 293, 295-358, 362, 364-397.
ANN (CINDY WILLIAMS)	1-9, 10-11, 12, 18, 19-22, 23-24, 25-26, 28, 58, 62, 66, 68, 71, 87, 103, 107, 182, 185, 222, 276-281, 282-283, 284, 285, 289, 291, 298, 299, 300-302, 303-304, 305, 306, 307-308, 309-316, 317-332, 356, 359-361, 363, 369-376.
MARK (FREDERIC FORREST)	1-9, 12, 18, 19-22, 23-24, 25-26, 58, 62, 66, 68, 71, 81, 87, 102, 103, 107, 182, 185, 222, 356, 359-361, 363, 369-376.
MR. "C" (ROBERT DUVALL)	206-221, 223-224, 356, 359-361, 363, 365.
STANLEY	12, 14-16, 27, 29, 51-57, 63, 67, 126-132, 137-142, 143, 144, 145, 146-149, 150 151-153, 154, 155, 156, 157-159.
PAUL	1-9, 19-22, 23-24, 27, 123, 126-132, 137-142, 143, 144, 145, 146-149, 150, 151-153, 154, 155, 156, 157-159, 222.
MARTIN	99, 100, 101, 102, 109-112, 113, 134-136, 137-142, 206-221, 223-224, 225, 369-376.
WILLIAM P. MORAN	126-132, 137-142, 143, 144, 145, 146-149, 150, 151-153, 154, 155, 156, 157-159, 161-173.
MEREDITH	126-132, 137-142, 143, 144, 145, 146-149, 150, 151-153, 154, 155, 156, 157-159, 160, 161-163, 174-181.
MILLARD	137-142, 143, 144, 145, 146-149, 150, 151-153, 154, 155, 156, 157-159, 161-173.
MRS. GOETNER	40, 44.
RON KELLER	
MRS. CORSITTO	
BOB	
BOB'S WIFE	
AMY	
LURLEEN	
MALE SECRETARY	
TONY	
MALE RECEPTIONIST	

CONTACT LIST
TOP SHEET

NOV. 24, 19--
DATE

PAGE 1 OF ____

FRANCIS FORD COPPOLA PRODS.
PRODUCTION COMPANY

THE CONVERSATION
PRODUCTION TITLE

____
PRODUCTION NO.

CONTACT	PAGE NO.	CONTACT	PAGE NO.	CONTACT	PAGE NO.
Airlines		Equipment		Office Supplies	
Airport		Film/Raw Stock		Pharmacy	
Art Supplies		Fire Dept.		Photography	
Ambulance		Florist		Police	
Bank		Food/Coffee/Water/Liquor		Payroll	
Beepers		Furniture Rental		Post Office	
Camera		Hardware		Prop Supplies	
Casting		Hospital		Production Office	
Cleaners		Hotels		Restaurants	
Copier/Dupe/Printing		Insurance		Studios	
Construction		Lumber Supplies		Telephone	
Custom Brokers		Mayor's Office of Film		Transportation	
Dailies/Lab		Messenger		Walkie-Talkies	
Dentist		Office Machines		Wardrobe	
Doctor		Office Maintenance		Weather	
Editorial					

CONTACT LIST

PAGE ______ OF ______

PRODUCTION TITLE: SAMPLE FEATURE

DATE: NOV. 23, 19--

AREA	CONTACT	TELEPHONE NO.
AIRLINES	AIR FRANCE (EMERG. PAGE 632-7157/7173)	247-0100
	AMERICAN	661-4242
	EASTERN	986-5000
	GOLDEN	466-0564
	TWA	290-2121
	UNITED	867-3000
	USAIR	736-3200
AIRPORT	TETERBORO, NEW JERSEY	201-288-1775
ART SUPPLIES	THE ART SUPPLIER 206 WEST 23RD. STREET NEW YORK, N.Y. 10017	687-9124
AMBULANCE		911
BANK	CITIBANK 141 EAST 23 ST. NEW YORK, N.Y. 10010	620-0011
BEEPERS	LIN COMMUNICATIONS (949-9400) 260 MADISON AVE. NEW YORK, N.Y. 10016	610-1936 610-4170 610-9939 610-4198 610-3004
CAMERA	GENERAL CAMERA CORP. 540 WEST 36 ST. NEW YORK, N.Y. 10018	594-8700
CASTING	CREATIVE CASTING NBC-30 ROCKEFELLER PL. NEW YORK, N.Y. 10022	666-6666
	EXTRAS SYLVIA FAY 71 PARK AVE. (5B) NEW YORK, N.Y. 10016	889-2626 889-2707
CLEANERS	PARKSIDE 66 LEXINGTON AVE. NEW YORK, N.Y. 10010	555-5555
COPIER/DUPE/PRINTING	XEROX CORPORATION 666 FIFTH AVENUE NEW YORK, N.Y. 10103	397-7100
	REPAIR SUPPLIES	736-0900 733-2000

CREW DEAL MEMO

FRANCIS FORD COPPOLA PRODS.
PRODUCTION COMPANY

THE CONVERSATION
PRODUCTION TITLE / NO.

NOV. 24, 19--
DATE

BOB HOTWIRE
EMPLOYEE NAME

456 ELECTRIC STREET
SAN FRANCISCO, CA 94000
EMPLOYEE ADDRESS

ELECTRICIAN
POSITION

123-45-6789
S.S. NO./EMPLOYER I.D. NO.

IATSE-LOCAL 728
UNION/GUILD

DEAL:

$14.68 / HOUR - 8 HOUR GUARANTEE

SAMPLE

ACCEPTED BY:

Bob Hotwire
EMPLOYEE'S SIGNATURE

APPROVED BY:

Clark Paylow
EXECUTIVE IN CHARGE OF PRODUCTION

CREW LIST

NOV. 24, 19- -
DATE

PAGE 1 OF 10

FRANCIS FORD COPPOLA PRODS.
PRODUCTION COMPANY

THE CONVERSATION
PRODUCTION TITLE

PRODUCTION NO.

POSITION	NAME AND ADDRESS	TELEPHONE NO.
PRODUCER/DIRECTOR WRITER	FRANCIS COPPOLA UNION SQUARE HOTEL UNION SQUARE SAN FRANCISCO, CA 94000	415-999-9999
PRODUCER	FRED ROOS UNION SQUARE HOTEL UNION SQUARE SAN FRANCISCO, CA 94000	415-999-9999
PRODUCER	MONA SKAGER UNION SQUARE HOTEL UNION SQUARE SAN FRANCISCO, CA 94000	415-999-9999
PRODUCTION MANAGER	CLARK PAYLOW UNION SQUARE HOTEL UNION SQUARE SAN FRANCISCO, CA 94000	415-999-9999
FIRST ASST. DIRECTOR	C. MEYERS UNION SQUARE HOTEL UNION SQUARE SAN FRANCISCO, CA 94000	415-999-9999
SECOND ASST. DIRECTOR	CONT'D.	

SAMPLE

CREW MOVEMENT LIST

THE CONVERSATION
PRODUCTION TITLE

DECEMBER 21, 19--
DATE

DAY OF THE WEEK	DATE	MOVEMENT INFORMATION — EXAMPLE: AIRLINE INFO; BUS; ETC. — INSTRUCTIONS
FRIDAY	12/22/--	PSA FLIGHT 123 - L.V. SFO 9:30 PM ARR. LA 10:30 PM

CREW MEMBERS NAME	POSITION
FRANCIS F. COPPOLA	DIR/WRITER/PRODUCER
MONA SKAGER	PRODUCER
FRED ROOS	PRODUCER

COMMENTS

LIMOS TO PICK-UP LUGGAGE AT UNION SQUARE HOTEL AT 7:30 PM THEN GO TO 765 MISSION ST. LOCATION. PICK-UP AT 8:00 PM. AND GO TO SFO INT'L AIRPORT.

DAY OF THE WEEK	DATE	MOVEMENT INFORMATION — EXAMPLE: AIRLINE INFO; BUS; ETC. — INSTRUCTIONS
SATURDAY	12/23/--	PSA FLIGHT 465 - LV. SFO 10AM ARR. LA 11:00 AM

CREW MEMBERS NAME	POSITION
CLARK PAYLOW	PROD'N MGR.
C. MEYERS	FIRST A.D.

COMMENTS

DRIVER TO PICK-UP AT UNION SQUARE HOTEL AT 8:15 AM TO SFO INT'L AIRPORT.

DAY OF THE WEEK	DATE	MOVEMENT INFORMATION — EXAMPLE: AIRLINE INFO; BUS; ETC. — INSTRUCTIONS

CREW MEMBERS NAME	POSITION

COMMENTS

DAILY CALL SHEET

F.F. COPPOLA / 415-999-9999	THE CONVERSATION	
PRODUCTION COMPANY/PHONE NO.	PRODUCTION TITLE	PRODUCTION NUMBER
MONDAY 11/27/--	2	7:00 AM
DAY / DATE	DAY NUMBER	CREW CALL
F.F. COPPOLA	C. MEYERS	
DIRECTOR	1ST ASSISTANT DIRECTOR	2ND ASSISTANT DIRECTOR

CAST	CHARACTER	MAKE-UP	ON SET	TRANSPORT
GENE HACKMAN	HARRY CAUL	7:00A	7:30A	P/U AT HOTEL 6:30AM

EXTRAS AND STANDINS		PROPS	SPECIAL INSTRUCTIONS
1 STAND-IN 25 EXTRAS (BUS DRIVER, COUNTER CLERK, ETC.)		PACKAGES BRIEFCASES, ETC. FOR PASSENGERS. (34, 35, 36) TOMATO, PORKCHOPS (IN CELLOPHANE), CAN OF BEER, MONEY, SACK PURCHASES (38)	SP.FX - SPARKS FROM BUS (34, 36

SAMPLE

SET NAME/ACTOR NO.	SCENES	PAGES	D/N	LOCATION
EXT.- ELECTRIC BUS (1)	34	1/8	D	} FILLMORE + HAYS ST.
EXT.- HARRY'S NEIGHBORHOOD (1)	36-37	2/8	D	}
INT. - ELECTRIC BUS (1)	35	2/8	D	- FILLMORE + HAYS ST.
INT. - NEIGHBORHOOD MARKET (1)	38	1/8	D	- YOUNG'S FOOD MART.

ADVANCE SCHEDULE	TRANSPORTATION
SC. 96 - EXT. FINANCIAL DISTRICT - DAY - 1/8 SC. 97 - EXT. FINANCIAL PLAZA - DAY 1/8 SC. 271-272 - EXT. FINANCIAL PLAZA - DAY - 2/8 SC. 282-283 - EXT. DIRECTOR'S BLDG. - DAY - 3/8	CHECK WITH TRANSPORTATION COORDINATOR.

COVER SET

SCS. 104, 105, 106, 108 - AMY'S APT. BLDG.

DAILY CALL SHEET—(Cont'd)

CREW CALL

Director	7A	Set Grips	7A	V.T.R. Crew	—	Trans. Coord.	6:30A	**Vehicles:**	
Choreographer	—	Rig Grips	—	Sound Mixer	7:00A	Trans. Capt.	6:30A	Camera Cars	
Dialogue Coach	—	Crane Grips	—	Boom Oper.	7:00A	Drivers	SEE CAPT.	Sound Wagon	
Stunt Coord.	—	Constr. Grips	—	Cable Men	7:00A	Editor	—	Camera Truck	
1st Asst. Dir.	7A	Scenic Grips	—	Playback	—	Asst. Editor	—	Electric Trucks	
2nd Asst. Dir.	6:45A	Scenic Chargeman	—	Gaffer	7:00A	Coffee	6:30A	Grip Trucks	
D.G.A. Trainee	6:45A	Scenic Artists	—	Set Elect.	7:00A	Caterer	6:30A	Prop Trucks	
P.A.'s (2)	7:00A	Set Standby Scenic	7:00A	Rig Elect.	—			Genny Trucks	
Script Super	7:00A	Greensmen	—	Genny Oper.	7:00A	**Equipment:**		Wardrobe Truck	
Loc. Mgr.	6:30A	Watchmen	—	Spec. Efx.	7:00A	Cameras	—	Add'l Trucks	
Prod. Auditor	—	Police (2)	6:30A	Set Dec.	6:00A	Zooms	—	Buses	
Tech. Advisor	—	Firemen	—	Leadman	6:00A	Booms	—	Station Wagons	
Prod. Designer	7:00A	First Aid/Nurse	7:00A	Swing Gang	—	Dollies	—	Cars	
Art Director	7:00A	Doctor	—	Wranglers	—	Cranes	—	Vans	
Set Designer	SEE ART DIR.	Dir. of Photo.	7:00A	Costume Des.	7:00A	Sound Channels	—	People Mover	
Sketch Artist	SEE ART DIR.	Camera Op.	7:00A	Wardrobe	6:42A	Playback/PA	—	Picture Cars	
Const. Coord.	6:00A	1st Asst. Cam.	7:00A	Make-up	6:42A	Projector	—	Trailers	
Carpenters	SEE CONST. COORD.	2nd Asst. Cam.	7:00A	Hair Dressers	6:42A	Arc Lamps	—	Portable Toilets	
Propmakers	" " "	Camera Trainee	7:00A	Prop Master	7:00A	Special Props	—	Honey Wagon	↓ SEE TRANSP. COORD.
Set Standby Carp.	7:00A	Still Camera	7:00A	Asst. Props	7:00A	Meals	SEE CATERER		
Key Grip	7:00A	Projectionist	—	Outside Props	7:00A	Portable Genny	—		

Notes:

DAILY PRODUCTION REPORT

FRANCIS FORD COPPOLA	THE CONVERSATION	
PRODUCTION COMPANY	PRODUCTION TITLE	PRODUCTION NUMBER
MONDAY – 11/27/– –	2	7:00 AM
DAY / DATE	SHOOTING DAY NUMBER	CREW CALL
8:15 AM	5:30 PM	6:00 PM
1st SHOT	LAST SHOT OF DAY	CREW WRAP
2:12 PM	F. F. COPPOLA	11/26/– –
1st SHOT AFTER LUNCH	DIRECTOR	START DATE
COPPOLA / ROOS / SKAGER	F. F. COPPOLA	1/30/– –
	PRODUCER	ESTIMATED FINISH DATE

PRODUCTION DAYS	SCHED. DAYS	ACTUAL DAYS
LOCAL LOCATIONS		
REHEARSAL DAYS	10	10
STUDIO DAYS	0	0
L. LOCATION DAYS	41	2
HOLIDAYS	2	0
IDLE DAYS	6	0
DISTANT LOCATIONS		
REHEARSAL DAYS	0	0
LOCATION DAYS	0	0
HOLIDAYS	0	0
IDLE DAYS	0	0
TRAVEL	0	0
TOTAL DAYS AHEAD OR BEHIND SCHEDULE	0	

SCRIPT LOG	PAGES	SCENES	ADDED SCENES	RETAKEN SCENES	SCRIPT NOTES
SCRIPT TOTAL	157	397	0	0	
SHOT BEFORE	3-4/8	15	0	0	—
SHOT TODAY	6/8	5	0	0	—
TOTAL SHOT TO DATE	4 2/8	20			—

MINUTES SHOT	BEFORE TODAY	TO DATE	SCENE NOS.
0:45	3:30	4:15	34, 36, 37, 35, 38

SOUND NOS. —

ADDED/RETAKES —

	FILM					STILLS	SOUND	
	DRAWN	EXPOSED	PRINT	N.G.	WASTE	35 MM STILLS	NO. 1/4" ROLLS	WILD-TRAX
BEFORE	25000	5000'	3000'	1500'	500'	4 RLS.	4 RLS.	0
TODAY	0	2000'	1200'	600'	200'	6 RLS.	2 RLS.	1
TO DATE	25000	7000'	4200'	2100'	700'	10 RLS.	6 RLS.	1

TOTAL SHOT INVENTORY	MEALS 1ST	2ND	3RD	PENALTIES
18000	1–1:30			NONE

SCENE NAME	LOCATION
34, 36, 37 EXT. STREET / ELECTRIC BUS / NEIGHBORHOOD — DAY	FILLMORE + HAYS STREETS
35 INT. ELECTRIC BUS / DAY	FILLMORE + HAYS STREETS
38 INT. MARKET / DAY	YOUNGS FOOD MART

REMARKS

LOST HALF-HOUR DUE TO PROBLEMS WITH ELECTRIC BUS.

C. MYERS	GOOD	C. PAYLOW
ASSISTANT DIRECTOR	WEATHER	PRODUCTION MANAGER

(OVER)

DAILY PRODUCTION REPORT—(Cont'd)

CAST MEMBERS	STATUS											
		TIME CALLED					HOURS			DAYS		
REHEARSE - R / STARTED - S / HOLD - H / TRAVEL - T / WORKED - W / ON CALL - C / FINISHED - F	W H S F R C	MAKE-UP WARD.	ON SET	MEALS	TRAVEL TIME	DIS-MISSED	ST.	1½	DBL.	WKD.	IDLE	TOTAL
GENE HACKMAN	W	7A	7:30A	1-1:30	0	5:45P	—	—	—	2	0	2
JOHN CAZALE	H	—	—	—	—	—	—	—	—	1	1	2
EXTRAS/STAND INS:												
1 STAND-IN	W	7A	7:30	1-1:30	0	5:30	8	1	0	—	—	—
20 EXTRAS	W	7A	7:30	1-1:30	0	5:30	8	1	0	—	—	—
5 EXTRAS	W	7A	7:30	1-1:30	0	4:30	8	0	0	—	—	—

CREW CALL

Director	7A	Set Grips	7A	V.T.R. Crew	—	Trans. Coord.	6:30A	**Vehicles:**	
Choreographer	—	Rig Grips	—	Sound Mixer	7A	Trans. Capt.	6:30A	Camera Cars	
Dialogue Coach	—	Crane Grips	—	Boom Oper.	7A	Drivers	SEE CAPT.	Sound Wagon	
Stunt Coord.	—	Constr. Grips	—	Cable Men	7A	Editor	—	Camera Truck	
1st Asst. Dir.	7A	Scenic Grips	—	Playback	—	Asst. Editor	—	Electric Trucks	
2nd Asst. Dir.	6:45A	Scenic Chargeman	—	Gaffer	7A	Coffee	6:30A	Grip Trucks	
D.G.A. Trainee	6:45A	Scenic Artists	—	Set Elect.	7A	Caterer	6:30A	Prop Trucks	
P.A.'s (2)	7:00 A	Set Standby Scenic	7A	Rig Elect.	—			Genny Trucks	
Script Super	7:00A	Greensmen	—	Genny Oper.	7A	**Equipment:**		Wardrobe Truck	
Loc. Mgr.	6:30A	Watchmen	—	Spec. Efx.	7A	Cameras	—	Add'l Trucks	
Prod. Auditor	—	Police (2)	6:30A	Set Dec.	6A	Zooms	—	Buses	
Tech. Advisor	—	Firemen	?	Leadman	6A	Booms	—	Station Wagons	
Prod. Designer	7:00A	First Aid/Nurse	7A	Swing Gang	—	Dollies	—	Cars	
Art Director	7:00A	Doctor	—	Wranglers	—	Cranes	—	Vans	
Set Designer	SEE ART DIR.	Dir. of Photo.	7A	Costume Des.	7A	Sound Channels	—	People Mover	
Sketch Artist	SEE ART DIR.	Camera Op.	7A	Wardrobe	6:42A	Playback/PA	—	Picture Cars	
Const. Coord.	6:00A	1st Asst. Cam.	7A	Make-up	6:42A	Projector	—	Trailers	
Carpenters	SEE CONST. CRD.	2nd Asst. Cam.	7A	Hair Dressers	6:42A	Arc Lamps	—	Portable Toilets	
Propmakers	" " "	Camera Trainee	7A	Prop Master	7A	Special Props	—	Honey Wagon	
Set Standby Carp.	7A	Still Camera	7A	Asst. Props	7A	Meals	SEE CATERER		
Key Grip	7A	Projectionist	—	Outside Props	7A	Portable Genny	—	SEE TRANSP. COORD.	

Notes:

DEVELOPMENT COSTS

MAY 19--
DATE

FRANCIS FORD COPPOLA PRODS.
PRODUCTION COMPANY

THE CONVERSATION
PRODUCTION TITLE/NO.

FRANCIS FORD COPPOLA
PRODUCER

FRANCIS FORD COPPOLA
DIRECTOR

ACCOUNT NO.	ACCOUNT NAME/DESCRIPTION		AMOUNT ($)
	Story		$ 5,000
	Screenplay		$ 45,000
	Script Preparation		
	Typing	$ 600	
	Duplication	$ 500	$ 1,100
	Budget Preparation		
	Script Breakdown &		
	Production Board		$ 3500
	Accounting		$ 1,900
	Legal		
	Incorporation	$ 1500	
	Contracts	$ 1,000	
	Other	$ 1,000	$ 3,500
	Travel & Entertainment		$ 1,500
	Office Overhead		$ 4,500
	Additional Expenses		$ 2,000
	Miscellaneous		$ 2,000
		Total	$ 70,000

EQUIPMENT RENTAL AGREEMENT

FRANCIS FORD COPPOLA PRODS. — PRODUCTION COMPANY
THE CONVERSATION — PRODUCTION TITLE / NO.
NOV. 24, 19-- — DATE

N. D. GRIP EQUIP. CO. — RENTING COMPANY
432 MAIN STREET
SAN FRANCISCO, CA 94000 — COMPANY ADDRESS
415-999-9999 — PHONE NO.

GARY GRIP — EMPLOYEE NAME
432 MAIN STREET
SAN FRANCISCO, CA 94000 — EMPLOYEE ADDRESS

KEY GRIP — POSITION
987-65-4321/95-12345 — S.S. NO./EMPLOYER I.D. NO.

BASIC GRIP PACKAGE; TUBE DOLLY TRACK; CAMERA MOUNTS — SEE ATTACHED INVENTORY SHEET

SAMPLE

EQUIPMENT

I, GARY GRIP, warrant that I am the owner of the above described equipment and that I have the right and/or authority to rent or lease same to FRANCIS F. COPPOLA PRODUCTION'S, and/or the Producer, Production entitled THE CONVERSATION.

Daily Rate/or Weekly Rate of $800. beginning on 11-26-- delivered to F.F. COPPOLA PRODS. premises on 11-23-- (Date).

I understand and agree that FRANCIS F. COPPOLA PRODUCTION'S, and/or the Producer shall have no responsibility or liability for the safekeeping of the equipment nor shall they be responsible or liable for the replacement of the equipment or any part thereof.

Gary Grip — RENTER'S SIGNATURE
C. Payton — APPROVAL

LOANOUT AGREEMENT

FRANCIS FORD COPPOLA PRODS. — PRODUCTION COMPANY
THE CONVERSATION — PRODUCTION TITLE / NO.
NOV. 24, 19-- — DATE

R.S. SMITH PRODS. INC. — LENDING COMPANY
9903 SANTA MONICA BLVD. BEVERLY HILLS, CA — COMPANY ADDRESS
274-4766 — PHONE NO.

ROBERT SMITH — EMPLOYEE NAME
(SAME AS ABOVE) — EMPLOYEE ADDRESS

FIRST ASST. DIRECTOR — POSITION
123-45-6789 / 95-12345 — S.S. NO./EMPLOYER I.D. NO.
DGA — UNION / GUILD

DEAL:

SCALE RATE:

PREP - $1684.

SHOOT - $1976.

WRAP - $1684.

ONE WEEK GUARANTEE.

SCREEN CREDIT - AS PER DGA CONTRACT.

Lending Corp. represents and warrants that it is a California corporation in good standing entitled to furnish all of the services of Employee to be furnished hereunder, that it is authorized to enter into this agreement, that it is a signatory to the Union or Guild agreement referred to above (and that Employee is a member in good standing of such Union or Guild), and that the foregoing shall remain so during the term of this agreement.

ACCEPTED:

By R. S. Smith Productions, Inc.
Its PRESIDENT

APPROVED:

C. Paylow
EXECUTIVE IN CHARGE OF PRODUCTION

The undersigned hereby acknowledges that he has read and is familiar with, and that he hereby endorses and approves, all of the provisions of the foregoing agreement and agrees to be bound thereby and to perform all of the terms and conditions thereof, insofar as the same are to be performed by him, in the same manner as if he had executed said agreement; and that he will look solely to Lending Corp. for all payments which may be due him under said agreement.

Robert Smith
EMPLOYEE'S SIGNATURE

PRODUCTION TITLE THE CONVERSATION Date NOV 26, 19--

LOCATION CREW CHECK LIST

TITLE	YES	NO	PER DIEM	HOTEL	MEALS	REMARKS
Executive Producer	✓		$1000.00			
Producer(S) 3	✓		3 x $1000.00			COPPOLA, ROOS, SKAGER
Associate Producer	✓		$1000.00			
Producer's Secretary		✓				
Director	✓		SEE PRODUCER			
Second Unit Director		✓				
Choreographer		✓				
Dialogue Director		✓				
Director's Secretary		✓				
Cast Members						
GENE HACKMAN	✓		$1000.00 WK.			
CINDY WILLIAMS	✓		$1000.00 WK.			
FREDERIC FORREST	✓		$1000.00 WK.			
Casting Director						
Welfare Worker/Teacher						
Stunt Coordinator						
Production Manager						
First Assistant Director						
Second Assistant Director						
Location Manager						
Production Accountant						
Assistant to Prod. Acct.						
DGA Trainee						
Production Assistants						
Script Supervisor						
Production Office Coordinator						
Production Secretary						
Technical Advisor						
Extra Casting Director						
Production Designer						
Art Director						
Assistant Art Director						
Set Designer						
Draftsman						
Sketch Artist						
Construction Coordinator						
Construction Foreman						
Set Decorator						
Swing Gang — Leadman						

(Continued on Next Page)

PRODUCTION TITLE ______________________ Date ______________

LOCATION CREW CHECK LIST

TITLE	YES	NO	PER DIEM	HOTEL	MEALS	REMARKS
Swing Gang — Second						
Greensman						
Painter						
Propmaster						
Asst. Propmaster						
Special Effects Foreman						
Special Effects — Add'l						
Director of Photography						
Camera Operator						
Additional Camera Operator						
1st Assistant Camera						
2nd Assistant Camera						
Special Camera Operator						
Camera Trainee						
Mixer						
Mike Boom Operator						
Cable Puller						
Key Grip						
2nd Company Grip						
Dolly Grip						
Crane Grip						
Company Grip						
Gaffer						
Best Boy						
Generator Operator						
Electricians						
Costume Designer						
Assistant to Costume Designer						
Women's Costumer						
Women's Costumer — Set						
Men's Costumer						
Men's Costumer — Set						
Tailor						
Seamstress						
Make-up Artist						
Make-up Assistant						
Body Make-up						
Hair Stylist						
Hair Stylist Assistant						
Transportation Coordinator						
Captain						
Co-Captain						
Drivers						

(Continued on Next Page)

PRODUCTION TITLE ______________________________ Date ____________________

LOCATION CREW CHECK LIST

TITLE	YES	NO	PER DIEM	HOTEL	MEALS	REMARKS
Editor						
Assistant Editor						
Video Tape Cameraman						
Video Monitor Operators						
Unit Publicist						
Still Photographer						

MEAL ALLOWANCE SHEET

DAY / DATE Monday, December 4, 19--
PRODUCTION TITLE THE CONVERSATION
PRODUCTION NO. ____________

DEPARTMENT GRIP

MEAL RATES
Breakfast $7.50
Lunch $15.00
Dinner $25.00

DAY	MON			TUE			WED			THU			FRI			SAT			SUN			TOTAL	NAME	SIGNATURE
DATE	11/27			11/28			11/29			11/30			12/1			12/2			12/3					
	B	L	D	B	L	D	B	L	D	B	L	D	B	L	D	B	L	D	B	L	D			
	✓		✓	✓		✓	✓		✓	✓		✓	✓		✓							$162.50	GARY GRIP	Gary Grip
	✓			✓		✓	✓			✓			✓		✓							$87.50	MIKE GRIP	Michael Grip
	✓		✓	✓		✓			✓			✓	✓		✓							$147.50	STU GRIP	Stu Grip
TOTAL																								

APPROVAL

PRODUCTION MANAGER C. Payton LOCATION AUDITOR Ima Stickler

ONE LINE SHOOTING SCHEDULE

FRANCIS FORD COPPOLA PRODS.	THE CONVERSATION	
PRODUCTION COMPANY	PRODUCTION TITLE	PRODUCTION NUMBER
FRANCIS F. COPPOLA	FRANCIS F. COPPOLA	NOV. 24, 19--
PRODUCER	DIRECTOR	DATE

DAY NO.	DAY/ DATE	INT/ EXT	SET NAME/ ONE LINE DESCRIPTION	D/N	SCENE NO.	TOTAL PAGES
1	SUN 11/26	EXT.	FINANCIAL DISTRICT HARRY GOES THROUGH SUNDAY STREETS, SIGNS IN AND GOES UP.	D	195-198	5/8
1	SUN 11/26	EXT.	FINANCIAL DISTRICT (PHONE BOOTH) HARRY AT LOOSE ENDS, GOES INTO PHONE BOOTH	D	226-229	4/8
1	SUN 11/26	EXT.	GOLDEN GATE PARK HARRY ACCOSTS STAN. TELLS HIM THAT MEREDITH STOLE THINGS AND TO STAY AWAY FROM HIM.	D	188-194	2-3/8
2	MON 11/27	EXT.	STREET ELECTRIC BUS TRAVELS UP STREET	D	34	1/8
2	MON 11/27	EXT.	ELECTRIC BUS DRIVER FIXES ROD - HARRY WALKS HOME	D	36	1/8

PER DIEM EXPENSE REPORT

FRANCIS FORD COPPOLA PRODS.	THE CONVERSATION	JANUARY 6, 19--
PRODUCTION COMPANY	PRODUCTION TITLE / NO.	DATE
DANIEL SINCLAIR	543-21-9876	D.G.A.
EMPLOYEE NAME	S.S. NO.	UNION / GUILD

DAY:	MONDAY	TUESDAY	WEDNESDAY	THURSDAY	FRIDAY	SATURDAY	SUNDAY	TOTAL
DATE:	12/18	12/19	12/20	12/21	12/22	12/23	12/24	
Transportation:								
Tickets	–	–	–	–	49 00	–	–	49.00
Local (taxi, carfare, etc.)	–	–	–	–	5 00	–	–	5.00
Baggage handling	–	–	–	–	4. 00	–	–	4.00
Room	35 00	35 00	35 00	35 00	35 00			175.00
Meals:								
Breakfast	7 50	7 50	7 50	7 50	7 50	7 50	– –	45.00
Lunch	–	–	– –	– –	– –	– –	– –	
Dinner	28 00	28 00	28 00	28 00	28 00	– –	– –	
Telephone	6 50	9 25	36 00	1 50	12 92	– –	– –	
Laundry	– –	– –	28 50	– –	– –	– –	– –	
Other	4 00	– –	– –	6 00	– –	– –	– –	
TOTAL	81 00	79 75	135 00					
DAILY ALLOWANCE (if any)								
"TOTAL" Less "DAILY ALLOWANCE"								

Daniel Sinclair
EMPLOYEE'S SIGNATURE

APPROVAL

PETTY CASH ADVANCE RECEIPT

FRANCIS FORD COPPOLA PRODS. — PRODUCTION COMPANY
THE CONVERSATION — PRODUCTION TITLE/NO.
NOV. 24, 19-- — DATE

LARRY LOCATION — EMPLOYEE'S NAME
PRODUCTION — DEPARTMENT
$500.00 — AMOUNT

FIVE HUNDRED AND NO/100 ———— DOLLARS
(WRITE IN AMOUNT)

PURPOSE CASH PAYMENTS TO ELEVATOR OPERATOR, ETC. AT LOCATION PARTIAL DEPOSIT ON LOCATION.

I hereby acknowledge receipt of said sum and hereby agree to provide receipts to document expenditures. I also hereby grant the Production Company authority to deduct any undocumented expenditures from my last pay check.

Larry Location — EMPLOYEE'S SIGNATURE
C. Payton — APPROVED
Larry Location — PAYMENT RECEIVED

SAMPLE

PETTY CASH ADVANCE RECEIPT

________ PRODUCTION COMPANY
________ PRODUCTION TITLE/NO.
________ DATE

________ EMPLOYEE'S NAME
________ DEPARTMENT
________ AMOUNT

________ DOLLARS
(WRITE IN AMOUNT)

PURPOSE ________

I hereby acknowledge receipt of said sum and hereby agree to provide receipts to document expenditures. I also hereby grant the Production Company authority to deduct any undocumented expenditures from my last pay check.

________ EMPLOYEE'S SIGNATURE
________ APPROVED
________ PAYMENT RECEIVED

PETTY CASH—EXPENSE REPORT

FRANCIS FORD COPPOLA — PRODUCTION COMPANY

THE CONVERSATION — PRODUCTION TITLE

PRODUCTION NUMBER

JOAN YOUNG — EMPLOYEE NAME

PRODUCTION — DEPARTMENT

1 — VOUCHER NUMBER

FROM DEC. 16 19 -- TO DEC. 23 19 -- PAID BY CHECK NO.

ENTERED	AUDITED	APPROVED	PAID

DATE		NO.	DESCRIPTION/PAYEE	PURPOSE	ACCT.	AMOUNT	
12	16	1	MACY'S DEPT. STORE	OFFICE X-MAS PARTY		23	75
12	19	2	JOE'S DRUG STORE	COFFEE-DONUTS-OFFICE		4	63
12	20	3	HALLMARK PARTY STORE	CUPS, PAPER GOODS, X-MAS PARTY		19	82
						49	20

SAMPLE

PETTY CASH ADVANCE RECEIVED	$ 0	RECEIPTS PAID	$
TOTAL RECEIPTS AND CASH	$ 49.20	CASH ON HAND	$
(OVER OR UNDER)	$ 49.20	TOTAL	$

DISTRIBUTION OF EXPENSES

										MISCELLANEOUS
										TOTALS

PETTY CASH REIMBURSEMENT RECEIPT

FRANCIS FORD COPPOLA PRODS. — PRODUCTION COMPANY
THE CONVERSATION — PRODUCTION TITLE/NO.
JANUARY 15, 19-- — DATE

JOAN YOUNG — EMPLOYEE'S NAME
PRODUCTION — DEPARTMENT
$49.20 — AMOUNT

FORTY-NINE AND 20/100 ______ DOLLARS
(WRITE IN AMOUNT)

EXPENSE REPORT DATED DECEMBER 23, 19--

Joan Young — EMPLOYEE'S SIGNATURE
C Panforo — APPROVED
J. Young — PAYMENT RECEIVED

PETTY CASH REIMBURSEMENT RECEIPT

SAMPLE

______ PRODUCTION COMPANY
______ PRODUCTION TITLE/NO.
______ DATE

______ EMPLOYEE'S NAME
______ DEPARTMENT
______ AMOUNT

______ DOLLARS
(WRITE IN AMOUNT)

EXPENSE REPORT DATED ______

______ EMPLOYEE'S SIGNATURE
______ APPROVED
______ PAYMENT RECEIVED

PHOTO RELEASE

FRANCIS FORD COPPOLA PRODS.	THE CONVERSATION	JULY 1, 19--
PRODUCTION COMPANY	PRODUCTION TITLE / NO.	DATE

I hereby give and grant to you the right to use my name and/or the right to photograph my physical likeness in any manner you desire and/or the right to reproduce and record my voice and other sound effects made by me, and I hereby consent to the use of my name and/or said photographs, likenesses and any reproductions thereof and/or the recordations and reproductions of my voice and other sound effects, by you, your licensees, successors and assigns, in or in connection with the production, exhibition, distribution, advertising and exploitation and/or other use of any of your photoplays and/or otherwise.

NAME	SIGNATURE	ADDRESS
JURI KOLL	Juri Koll	123 ELM STREET, SAN FRANCISCO, CA
GLORIANE HARRIS	Gloriane Harris	456 GREEN STREET, SAN FRANCISCO, CA
KAREN GINSBERG	Karen Ginsberg	425 CORTE STRADA, SAN RAFAEL, CA
WM EUSTACE	Wm. Eustace	2020 WEST AVENUE, SAN FRANCISCO, CA
BILL HASSELL	Bill Hassell	657 MAIN STREET, SAN FRANCISCO, CA
PATRICK DALY	Patrick Daly	523 FIFTH STREET, SAN FRANCISCO, CA
DAVID SIEGEL	David Siegel	501 NORTH AVENUE, SAN FRANCISCO, CA

PRODUCERS BUDGETARY TOP SHEET

DATE: NOV. 24, 19--

FRANCIS FORD COPPOLA PRODS.	THE CONVERSATION	
PRODUCTION COMPANY	PRODUCTION TITLE	PRODUCTION NO.
FRANCIS F. COPPOLA	FRANCIS F. COPPOLA	NOV. 22, 19--
PRODUCER	DIRECTOR	SCRIPT DATE
NOV. 26, 19--	JAN. 30, 19--	JUL. 1, 19--
START DATE	FINISH DATE	ANSWER PRINT DATE

SHOOTING SCHEDULE	FIRST UNIT	SECOND UNIT
LOCAL LOCATION		
Rehearsal Days	10	0
Studio Days	0	0
Local Location Days	41	0
Holidays	2	0
Idle Days	6	0
Travel Days	0	0
DISTANT LOCATION		
Rehearsal Days	0	0
Location Days	0	0
Holidays	0	0
Idle Days	0	0
Travel Days	0	0
TOTAL DAYS	59	0

TOTAL BUDGET

APPROVED BY: Francis Ford Coppola (PRODUCER) Francis Ford Coppola (DIRECTOR)

PRODUCTION COST REPORT

PAGE NO. 1

FEATURE FILMS INC.
PRODUCTION COMPANY

SAMPLE FEATURE
PRODUCTION TITLE / NO.

4/7/--
PERIOD ENDING

ACCT. NO.	ACCOUNT NAME	ORIGINAL BUDGET	TO DATE	ESTIMATED COST TO COMPLETE	ESTIMATED FINAL COST	(OVER) UNDER BUDGET	COMMENTS
1000	Story and Screenplay	156,250	144,446	-0-	144,446	11,804	
1100	Producers Unit	233,500	111,650	121,850	233,500	-0-	
1200	Directors Unit	255,600	112,108	143,492	255,600	-0-	
1300	Cast Unit	937,050	319,280	634,670	953,950	(16,900)	
1400	Travel and Living Unit	100,100	82,419	17,681	100,100	-0-	
1900	Fringe Benefits & Payroll Taxes	444,147	4,621	439,526	444,147	-0-	
TOTAL ABOVE THE LINE BUDGET		2,126,647	774,524	1,357,219	2,131,743	(5,096)	
2000	Production Department	110,855	87,766	40,089	127,855	(17,000)	
2100	Extra Talent	100,862	22,942	120,980	143,922	(43,060)	
2200	Art Department	73,200	55,890	27,260	83,150	(9,950)	
2300	Set Construction	130,800	85,341	47,309	132,650	(1,850)	
2400	Set Dressing	86,997	51,045	24,952	75,997	11,000	
2500	Property	41,251	23,922	25,079	49,001	(7,750)	
2600	Picture Vehicles	35,700	19,280	16,420	35,700	-0-	
2700	Special Effects	19,220	11,841	10,379	22,220	(3,000)	
2800	Camera	113,529	60,273	58,806	119,079	(5,550)	

(Continued on Next Page)

PRODUCTION COST REPORT

PAGE NO. 2

FEATURE FILMS INC.
PRODUCTION COMPANY

SAMPLE FEATURE
PRODUCTION TITLE/NO.

4/7/- -
PERIOD ENDING

ACCT. NO.	ACCOUNT NAME	ORIGINAL BUDGET	TO DATE	ESTIMATED COST TO COMPLETE	ESTIMATED FINAL COST	(OVER) UNDER BUDGET	COMMENTS
3000	Special Equipment	—	—	—			
3100	Sound	37,250	24,452	12,798			
3200	Grip	63,645	27,560	36,085			
3300	Lighting	67,315	41,876	25,439			
3400	Wardrobe	71,360	37,275	34,085			
3500	Make-up and Hair	49,893	18,718	49,275			
3600	Set Operations	95,875	87,560	15,000			
3700	Site Rental	37,250	12,798	24,452			
3800	Stage Expense	—	—	—			
4000	Location Expense	91,713	69,752	34,961			
4100	Second Unit	—	—	—			
4200	Tests	5,000	152	9,696			

SAMPLE

(Continued on Next Page)

PRODUCTION COST REPORT

PAGE NO. 3

FEATURE FILMS INC.
PRODUCTION COMPANY

SAMPLE FEATURE
PRODUCTION TITLE/NO.

4/7/- -
PERIOD ENDING

ACCT. NO.	ACCOUNT NAME	ORIGINAL BUDGET	TO DATE	ESTIMATED COST TO COMPLETE	ESTIMATED FINAL COST	(OVER) UNDER BUDGET	COMMENTS
4300	Miniatures	—	—	—			
4400	Process	2,500	188	2,312			
4500	Animals	—	—	—			
4600	Transportation	214,629	156,035	95,094			
4700	Rawstock/Laboratory	58,084	35,066	34,961			
4900	Fringe Benefits & Payroll Taxes	282,223	337,280	226,943			
TOTAL BELOW THE LINE BUDGET		792,151					
5000	Film Editing	78,700	14,414	66,786			
5100	Music	95,000	-0-	95,000			
5200	Film Effects	10,000	—	10,000			
5300	Titles	10,000	274	9,726			
5400	Post Production Sound	31,020	1,593	29,427			
5500	Post Production Film	18,445	-0-	184,445			
5900	Fringe Benefits & Payroll Taxes	45,969	770	45,199			
TOTAL POST PRODUCTION BUDGET		203,634					

(Continued on Next Page)

PRODUCTION COST REPORT

PAGE NO. 4

FEATURE FILMS INC.
PRODUCTION COMPANY

SAMPLE FEATURE
PRODUCTION TITLE / NO.

4/7/- -
PERIOD ENDING

ACCT. NO.	ACCOUNT NAME	ORIGINAL BUDGET	TO DATE	ESTIMATED COST TO COMPLETE	ESTIMATED FINAL COST	(OVER) UNDER BUDGET	COMMENTS
6000	Publicity	46,625	26,503	24,622			
6100	Insurance	72,140	45,953	45,187			
6200	General Expense	46,634	9,020	37,614			
6900	Fringe Benefits & Payroll Taxes	289,134	17,051	274,583			
TOTAL OTHER COSTS		454,533					
TOTAL DIRECT COSTS		4,576,965					
7500	Contingency	457,696.50					
7600	Completion Bond	302,079.70					
7700	Overhead	—					
7800	Interest	—					
TOTAL NEGATIVE COSTS		5,336,741.19					
8000	Deferments	—					
TOTAL NEGATIVE COSTS (incl. Deferments)		$5,336,741.19					

SAMPLE

PRODUCTION CHECKLIST

DATE: *NOVEMBER 24, 19--*

FRANCIS FORD COPPOLA PRODS.
PRODUCTION COMPANY

THE CONVERSATION
PRODUCTION TITLE / NO.

CAST—SPEAKING	
Deal Memos	✓
Contracts Signed	✓
Wardrobe Fitted	✓
Special Make-up	N/A
Hair Falls or Wigs	N/A
Stunt/Photo Doubles	✓
Minors—Intent to Employ	✓
Welfare Worker/Teacher *TONY - SCS. 93, 94-95*	✓
SAG—Station 12 Checked	✓
Musicians	✓
Other:	
CREW—CAMERA	
Equipment Ordered/Checked	✓
Film Ordered	✓
Dolly Needed	✓
Other: *SECOND CAMERA FOR 1st 10*	✓
DAYS OF SHOOTING	
CREW—SOUND	
Equipment Ordered/Checked	✓
1/4" Tape Ordered	✓
Walkie Talkies	✓
PA System	✓
Playback	✓
Communication System to Set	✓
Other:	
CREW—OTHER	
Art Director—	✓
Grips—Any Special Equipment	✓
Electricians—Light Changes	✓
Special Effects—Discuss & Set	✓
Props—Discuss	✓
Make-up—Period/Special	
Body Make-up	
Hair—Period/Special	
Wardrobe—Period/Special	
Greensman—Special	
Script Supervisor—Script Timing	
Dialogue Coach	
Transportation Coordinator—Period/Special	
Set Decorator—Period/Special	
Other:	

SILENT—ATMOSPHERE	
Interviews	
Fittings	
Vouchers	
Mileage	
Minors—Intent to Employ	
Welfare Worker/Teacher	
Make-up or Hair—Period/Special	
Adjustments Necessary	
Piano Player for Music Cues	
Other:	
MISCELLANEOUS	
Technical Advisors	
First Aid	
Police	
Guards	
Firemen & Fire Permits	
City License/Permits	
Location Permits	
Heaters	
Livestock or Animals	
Handlers or Wranglers	
Tables and Benches	
Schoolroom Facilities	
Coffee & Rolls	
Breakfast	
Lunch	
Dinner	
Call Sheets	
Set Status Reports	
Production Reports	
Transportation and Lunch Lists	
Other:	
EQUIPMENT	
Generator	
Extra Camera	
Crane	
Special Process	
Trucks	
Vehicles—Picture or Standby	
Buses	
Insert Car	
Water Wagon	
Honeywagons	
Dressing Rooms	
Motor Homes	
Other:	

PRODUCTION REPORT SUMMARY
TOP SHEET

FRANCIS FORD COPPOLA PRODS.	THE CONVERSATION	
PRODUCTION COMPANY	PRODUCTION TITLE	PRODUCTION NO.
MONDAY - 11-27-	2	7:00 AM
SHOOTING DAY/DATE	SHOOTING DAY NO.	CREW CALL
8:15 AM	5:30 PM	6:00 PM
1ST SHOT OF DAY	LAST SHOT OF DAY	CREW WRAP

	SETUPS	SCENES	MINUTES	PAGES
PREVIOUS	20	15	3:30	3 - 4/8
TODAY	5	5	:45	6/8
TOTAL	25	20	4:15	4 - 2/8

NEIGHBORHOOD MARKET
LOCATIONS COMPLETED TODAY

34, 36, 37, 35, 38
SCENES COMPLETED TODAY

GENE HACKMAN, JOHN CAZALE
ACTORS WORKED

FINAL COMMENTS

LOST HALF-HOUR DUE TO PROBLEMS WITH
ELECTRIC BUS.

PRODUCTION GRATUITIES FORM

PRODUCTION TITLE THE CONVERSATION NO. ______ DATE JANUARY 31, 19--

DATE	ITEM	AMOUNT
12/27/--	A+P PARKING LOT - LOSS OF BUSINESS DUE TO FILMING.	$100.00
12/10/--	GARBAGE MEN — REHEARSAL SPACE — CLEANED AND PICKED UP.	40.00
12/12/--	CHAMPAGNE — F. MENDELSSOHN - CHRISTMAS GIFT	16.04
12/22/--	TIP FOR SECURITY GUARDS	15.00
1/4/--	ELEVATOR OPERATOR - 4 DAYS	135.00

SAMPLE

CODE — BREAKDOWN SHEETS/STRIPS
Day Ext. — Yellow
Night Ext. — Green
Day Int. — White
Night Int. — Blue
Numbers refer to budget categories

SCRIPT BREAKDOWN SHEET

DATE: NOV. 24, 19--

PRODUCTION COMPANY: FRANCIS FORD COPPOLA PRODS.
PRODUCTION TITLE/NO.: THE CONVERSATION
BREAKDOWN PAGE NO.: 51
SCENE NO.: 51
SCENE NAME: HARRY'S WAREHOUSE - OFFICE
INT. OR EXT.: INT.
DESCRIPTION: HARRY + STANLEY TALK
DAY OR NIGHT: DAY
PAGE COUNT: 6/8

CAST Red (1301-2-3)	STUNTS Orange (1304-5)	EXTRAS/ATMOSPHERE Green (2120)
HARRY STANLEY		
	EXTRAS/SILENT BITS Yellow (2120)	
SPECIAL EFFECTS Blue (2700)	PROPS Violet (2500) BENCHES ELECTRONIC SURVEILLANCE EQUIPMENT CABINETS + SHELVES OLD SOFA MAGAZINE THREE PROF. TAPE RECORDERS MANILA ENVELOPE - SEVERAL PHOTOS	VEHICLES/ANIMALS Pink (2600/4500)
WARDROBE Circle (3400)	MAKE-UP/HAIR Asterisk (3500)	SOUND EFFECTS/MUSIC Brown (5100,5300,5400)
SPECIAL EQUIPMENT Box	PRODUCTION NOTES 1. TECH ADVISOR - SURVEILLANCE EQUIP. 2. COAT - HARRY 3. SEVERAL PHOTOS OF ANN AND MARK 8x10 B+W TAKEN FROM SURVEILLANCE SCENE IF SHOT FIRST - OTHERWISE MUST BE STAGED. (SCHEDULE STILL SESSION)	

SAMPLE

A blank sample is on page 293.

SCRIPT SUPERVISOR'S REPORT

SERIES: ______ PROD. NO.: ______

TITLE: THE CONVERSATION DATE: MONDAY - NOV. 27, 19--

SHOOTING DAY: 2 CREW CALL: 7:00 AM

1ST SHOT A.M.: 8:15 AM LUNCH 1:00 PM TILL 1:30 PM

1ST SHOT P.M.: 2:12 PM DINNER N/A TILL N/A

LAST SHOT: 5:30 PM WRAP: 6:00 PM

SCENES TODAY: 34, 36, 37, 35, 38

ADDED SCENES: N/A

RETAKES: N/A

	SCENES	PAGES	MINUTES	SETUPS	ADDED SCENES	RETAKES
In Script	397	157	110:00		N/A	N/A
Taken Previously	15	3-4/8	3:30		N/A	N/A
Taken Today	5	6/8	0:45		N/A	N/A
Taken To Date	20	4-2/8	4:15		N/A	N/A
To Be Taken	377	152-6/8	105:45		N/A	N/A

REMARKS: LOST ONE HALF-HOUR DUE TO PROBLEMS WITH ELECTRIC BUS.

SCRIPT SUPERVISOR'S SIGNATURE: Sally Stryd

SCRIPT SUPERVISOR'S REPORT

SERIES: ______ PROD. NO.: ______

TITLE: ______ DATE: ______

SHOOTING DAY: ______ CREW CALL: ______

1ST SHOT A.M.: ______ LUNCH ______ TILL ______

1ST SHOT P.M.: ______ DINNER ______ TILL ______

LAST SHOT: ______ WRAP: ______

SCENES TODAY: ______

ADDED SCENES: ______

RETAKES: ______

	SCENES	PAGES	MINUTES	SETUPS	ADDED SCENES	RETAKES
In Script						
Taken Previously						
Taken Today						
Taken To Date						
To Be Taken						

REMARKS: ______

SCRIPT SUPERVISOR'S SIGNATURE: ______

SET STATUS REPORT

FRANCIS FORD COPPOLA PRODS.	THE CONVERSATION	MONDAY - NOV. 27, 19--
PRODUCTION COMPANY	PRODUCTION TITLE/NO.	DAY/DATE

CREW CALL: 7:00AM
1ST SHOT: 8:15 AM
LUNCH: 1:00 - 1:30PM
1ST SHOT: 2:12 PM

DINNER: N/A
1ST SHOT: N/A
FINISH: 5:30 PM
OUT: 6:00 PM

REPORT NO.	TIME	SCENE NO.	SETUPS COMPLETED	SCENE/NAME/REMARKS
1	8:15A	34	1	FIRST SHOT
2	10:00A	36	2	PROBLEMS WITH ELECTRICAL SPARKS -
				SPECIAL EFFECTS
3	11:15A	37	3	MOVED INTO INTERIOR OF BUS.

SAMPLE

STUNT BREAKDOWN FORM

FRANCIS FORD COPPOLA PRODS.	THE CONVERSATION	
PRODUCTION COMPANY	PRODUCTION TITLE	PRODUCTION NO.
FRANCIS COPPOLA	FRANCIS COPPOLA	CLARK PAYLOW
PRODUCER	DIRECTOR	PRODUCTION MGR.
VIC STUNTMAN	NOV. 22, 19--	11/24/--
STUNT COORDINATOR	SCRIPT DATE	DATE

SCENE NAME(S) EXT. STREET - BURNING CAR

SCENE NO.(S) 365

SCENE DESCRIPTION MR. C. AND HIS MERCEDES BENZ GO UP IN FLAMES.

CAST/STUNT PERSON ROBERT DUVALL / SANDY STUNTMAN

EQUIPMENT DESCRIPTION **PROVIDED BY**

1. USED MERCEDES (1) — TRANSPORTATION
2. RUBBER CEMENT — EFFECTS
3. PROPANE GAS W/ FANTAIL BURNERS — SPECIAL EFFECTS
4. DUMMY — PROPS
5. WATER TANKER — CITY
6. UNIFORMED SAFETY OFFICER — CITY
7. SPECIAL EFFECTS PERSON — CLASS ONE CARD — CREW

RIGGING

FANTAIL BURNERS REQUIRE SEVERAL HOURS TO SET UP.

UNIT PRODUCTION MANAGER AND ASSISTANT DIRECTOR DEAL MEMORANDUM

This confirms our agreement to employ you on the film project described below as follows:

PATRICK PRODUCTION MANAGER
NAME

123-45-6789
S.S. NO./EMPLOYER I.D. NO.

LOS ANGELES, CA 90028
ADDRESS

213/999-9999
TELEPHONE

☑ UNIT PRODUCTION MANAGER
☐ FIRST ASSISTANT DIRECTOR
☐ SECOND ASSISTANT DIRECTOR
☐ ADDITIONAL SECOND ASSISTANT DIRECTOR

☑ THEATRICAL MOTION PICTURE
☐ TELEVISION MOTION PICTURE

SAMPLE

TITLE: THE CONVERSATION

SALARY: $1689. ☑ per week ☐ per day

START DATE: OCT 1, 19--

GUARANTEED PERIOD: ONE ☑ week(s) ☐ day(s)

and shall be prorated thereafter.

PRODUCTION FEE: $422.

☐ STUDIO ☑ DISTANT LOCATION ☐ COMBINATION

The undersigned reserves the right to terminate the employee at any time, subject only to the obligation to pay the balance of any compensation due, pursuant to Sections 7-1403, 13-206 and other applicable provisions of the DGA Basic Agreement of 1978, to which this employment is subject.

FRANCIS FORD COPPOLA PRODS.
Signatory Company

DATE: NOV. 24, 19--

By Francis Ford Coppola

WORLD TIME CHART

Add or subtract number of hours to Los Angeles time—Standard/Daylight		
Argentina +5/ +4	Holland +9/ +8	Phillipines +16/ +15
Australia +19[a]/ +17	India +13½/ +12½	Portugal +8[f]/ +8[g]
Austria +9/ +8	Indonesia +15/ +14	Puerto Rico +4/ +3
Belgium +9/ +8	Iran +11½/ +10½	Singapore +15½/ +14½
Brazil +5/ +4	Iraq +11/ +10	South Africa +10/ +9
Burma +14½/ +13½	Ireland +8/ +8	Spain +10/ +9
Chile +4/ +3	Israel +10/ +9	Sweden +9/ +8
Columbia +3/ +2	Italy +9/ +8[d]	Switzerland +9/ +8
Denmark +9/ +8	Japan +17/ +16	Taiwan +16/ +16
Dominican Republic +3/ +3	Lebanon +10/ +9	Thailand +15/ +14
Ecuador +3/ +2	Malaysia +15½/ +14½	Trinidad +4/ +3
Egypt +10/ +10[b]	Mexico +2/ +1	Uruguay +5/ +4
Finland +10/ +9	New Zealand +21[e]/ +19	Venezuela +4/ +3
France +9/ +8	Norway +9/ +8	Vietnam +16/ +15
Germany +9/ +8	Pakistan +13/ +12	
Great Britain +8/ +8	Panama +3/ +2	
Greece +10/ +10[c]	Paraguay +4/ +3	
Hong Kong +16/ +16	Peru +3/ +2	

Daylight Savings Time = last Sunday in April — last Sunday in October

a = +18 — 1st Sun/March — last Sun/April
b = +9 — last Sun/Sept. — last Sun/Oct.
c = +9 — 2nd Sun/Sept. — last Sun/Oct.
d = +9 — 1st Sun/June — last Sun/Sept.
e = +20 — 1st Sun/March — last Sun/April
f = +9 — last Sun/March — last Sun/April
g = +7 — last Sun/Sept. — last Sun/Oct.

The Conversation - Scene Number/Day Number

In the event you want to find out when a particular scene was scheduled, and you don't want to go through the entire Shooting Schedule in **Film Scheduling**, this index will provide a quick, easy reference.

SCENE NO.	DAY(S)	SCENE NO.	DAY(S)	SCENE NO.	DAY(S)	SCENE NO.	DAY(S)
1	5/6	41	18	81	7	120 (pt.)	21
2	5/6	42	19	82	30/31	121	40
3	5/6	43	19	83	30/31	122	40
4	5/6	44	19	84	30/31	123 (pt.)	40
5	5/6	45	3	85	30/31	123 (pt.)	21
6	5/6	46	11	86	30/31	124	40
7	5/6	47	11	87	5/6	125	21
8	5/6	48	20	88	30/31	126	41
9	5/6	49	20	89	30/31	127	41
10	8/9	50	30/31	90	30/31	128	41
11	8/9	51	30/31	91	30/31	129	41
12	10	52	30/31	92	21	130	41
13	8/9	53	30/31	93	17	131	41
14	10	54	30/31	94	17	132	41
15	10	55	30/31	95	17	133	39
16	10	56	30/31	96	4	134	39
17	8/9	57	30/31	97	4	135	39
18	8/9	58	5/6	98	13	136	39
19	7	59	30/31	99	15	137	39
20	7	60	30/31	100	15	138	39
21	7	61	30/31	101	15	139	39
22	7	62	5/6	102	15	140	39
23	8/9	63	30/31	103	8/9	141	39
24	8/9	64	5/6	104	12	142	39
25	8/9	65	30/31	105	12	143	39
26	8/9	66	5/6	106	12	144	38
27	10	67	30/31	107	5/6	145	38
28	7	68	5/6	108	12	146	38
29	10	69	30/31	109	40	147	38
30	8/9	70	30/31	110	40	148	38
31	8/9	71	5/6	111	40	149	38
32	8/9	72	30/31	112	40	150	38
33	7	73	30/31	113	40	151	38
34	2	74	30/31	114	40	152	38
35	2	75	30/31	115	40	153	38
36	2	76	30/31	116	40	154	38
37	2	77	30/31	117	40	155	38
38	2	78	30/31	118	40	156	38
39	21	79	30/31	119	40	157	38
40	18	80	30/31	120 (pt.)	40	158	38

SCENE NO.	DAY(S)	SCENE NO.	DAY(S)	SCENE NO.	DAY(S)	SCENE NO.	DAY(S)
159	38	219	16	279	13	339	37
160	32/33/34	220	16	280	13	340	37
161	32/33/34	221	16	281	13	341	37
162	32/33/34	222	7	282	4	342	37
163	32/33/34	223	16	283	4	343	37
164	32/33/34	224	16	284	26/27	344	37
165	32/33/34	225	16	285	26/27	345	37
166	32/33/34	226	1	286	26/27	346	37
167	32/33/34	227	1	287	26/27	347	37
168	32/33/34	228	1	288	26/27	348	37
169	32/33/34	229	1	289	26/27	349	37
170	32/33/34	230	21	290	26/27	350	37
171	32/33/34	231	21	291	26/27	351	37
172	32/33/34	232	22	292	26/27	352	37
173	32/33/34	233	22	293	26/27	353	37
174	35/36	234	22	294	26/27	354	24
175	35/36	235	22	295	26/27	355	37
176	35/36	236	22	296	26/27	356	25
177	35/36	237	22	297	26/27	357	37
178	35/36	238	22	298	26/27	358	37
179	35/36	239	23	299	26/27	359	25
180	35/36	240	23	300	26/27	360	25
181	35/36	241	23	301	26/27	361	25
182	7	242	23	302	26/27	362	37
183	35/36	243	23	303	26/27	363	25
184	35/36	244	23	304	26/27	364	37
185	7	245	23	305	26/27	365	3
186	35/36	246	23	306	26/27	366	13
187	35/36	247	23	307	26/27	367	13
188	1	248	23	308	26/27	368	13
189	1	249	23	309	28	369	14
190	1	250	23	310	28	370	14
191	1	251	23	311	28	371	14
192	1	252	23	312	28	372	14
193	1	253	23	313	28	373	14
194	1	254	22	314	28	374	14
195	1	255	24	315	28	375	14
196	1	256	24	316	28	376	14
197	1	257	24	317	28	377	20
198	1	258	24	318	28	378	20
199	13	259	24	319	28	379	20
200	14	260	24	320	28	380	29
201	14	261	24	321	28	381	29
202	14	262	24	322	28	382	29
203	14	263	24	323	28	383	29
204	14	264	24	324	28	384	29
205	14	265	24	325	28	385	29
206	16	266	24	326	28	386	29
207	16	267	24	327	28	387	29
208	16	268	24	328	28	388	29
209	16	269	24	329	28	389	29
210	16	270	24	330	28	390	29
211	16	271	4	331	28	391	29
212	16	272	4	332	28	392	29
213	16	273	14	333	37	393	29
214	16	274	14	334	37	394	29
215	16	275	14	335	37	395	29
216	16	276	13	336	37	396	29
217	16	277	13	337	37	397	29
218	16	278	13	338	37		

INDEX

CODE — BREAKDOWN SHEETS/STRIPS
Day Ext. — Yellow
Night Ext. — Green
Day Int. — White
Night Int. — Blue
Numbers refer to budget categories

SCRIPT BREAKDOWN SHEET

DATE

PRODUCTION COMPANY | PRODUCTION TITLE/NO. | BREAKDOWN PAGE NO.

SCENE NO. | SCENE NAME | INT. OR EXT.

DESCRIPTION | DAY OR NIGHT

PAGE COUNT

CAST Red (1301-2-3)	**STUNTS** Orange (1304-5) **EXTRAS/SILENT BITS** Yellow (2120)	**EXTRAS/ATMOSPHERE** Green (2120)
SPECIAL EFFECTS Blue (2700)	**PROPS** Violet (2500)	**VEHICLES/ANIMALS** Pink (2600/4500)
WARDROBE Circle (3400)	**MAKE-UP/HAIR** Asterisk (3500)	**SOUND EFFECTS/MUSIC** Brown (5100,5300,5400)
SPECIAL EQUIPMENT Box	**PRODUCTION NOTES**	

NOTES

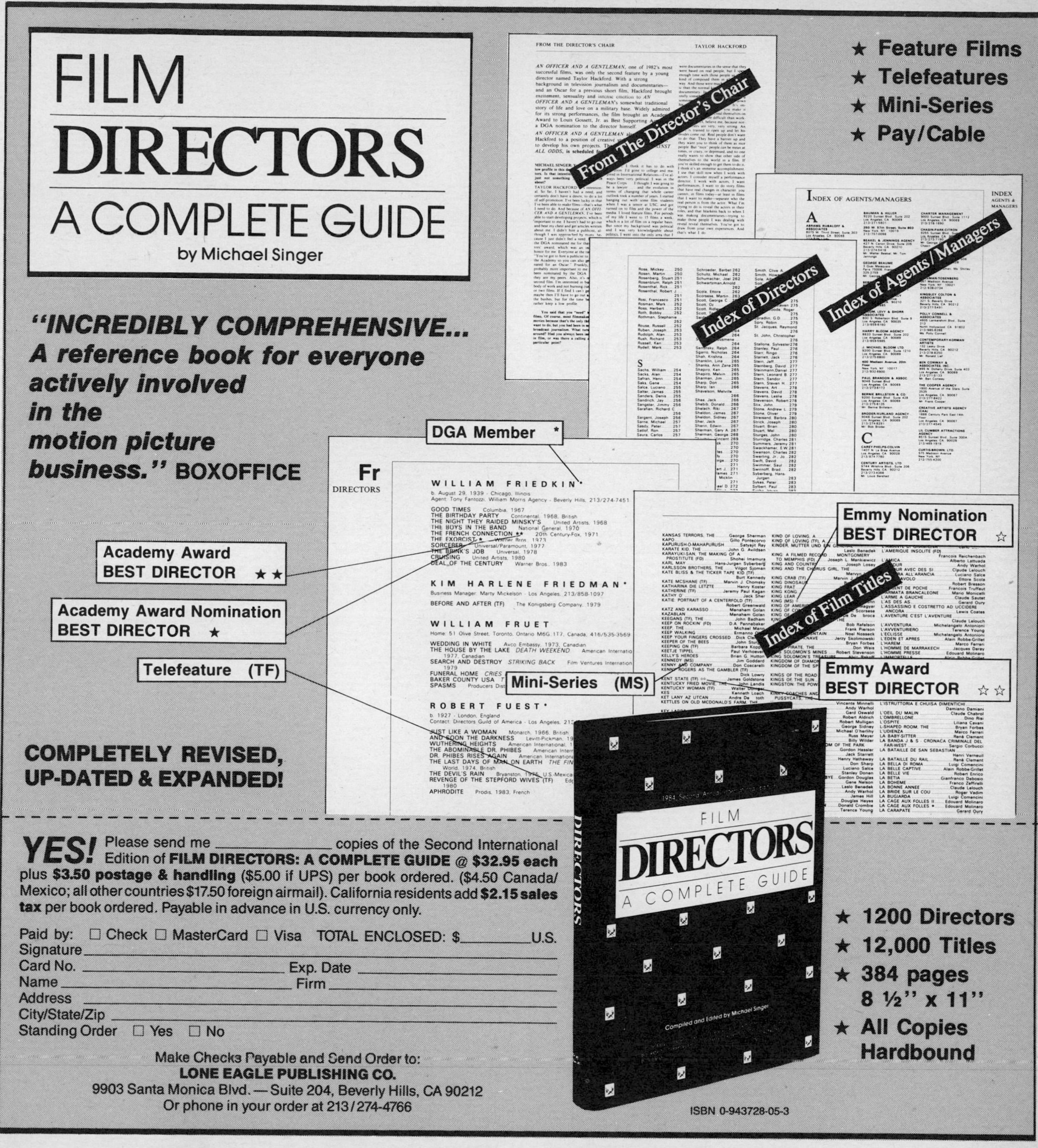

Updated annually. . .
Price subject to change without notice.

HOW TO ORDER MORE COPIES:

All Lone Eagle books are available from your local bookstores, or directly from the publisher.

Call 213/274-4766

or send check or money order for full amount in US funds plus $1.50 per order shipping/handling. Don't forget to add 6½% sales tax if shipped to California. We also accept Visa and MasterCard. Please include card number and expiration date. Allow 4-6 weeks for delivery. All prices subject to change without notice.

Lone Eagle Publishing
9903 Santa Monica Blvd. #204
Beverly Hills, CA 90212

ABOUT THE AUTHOR

Ralph S. Singleton works in the motion picture industry as a Production Manager / Assistant Director. He was head of production for Zoetrope Studios and was Production Manager on *Exposed* (MGM/UA), *One From The Heart* (Paramount), *The Winds of War* (USA-Paramount), *History of the World-Part I* (20th Century Fox), *Somebody Killed Her Husband* (Paramount), *Cagney & Lacey* (Orion), *Kojak* (Universal), etc.

He was also an Assistant Director on *Testament* (Paramount), *The Seduction of Joe Tynan* (20th Century Fox), *Greased Lightning* (Warner Bros.), *Taxi Driver* (Columbia), *Network* (Paramount), *The Front* (Warner Bros.), *Three Days of the Condor* (Paramount), *The Gambler* (Paramount), etc.

He is the only Assistant Director in the history of the Directors Guild of America to work on two Academy Award nominated films in the same year, and be nominated for the prestigious DGA award for both — *Network* and *Taxi Driver*. He is considered to be "one of the best production managers in the business." Mr. Singleton makes his home in Los Angeles, California.